D1559540

MINORITY GROUP THREAT, CRIME, AND POLICING

Minority Group Threat, Crime, and Policing

SOCIAL CONTEXT AND SOCIAL CONTROL

Pamela Irving Jackson

PRAEGER

New York
Westport, Connecticut
London

Library of Congress Cataloging-in-Publication Data

Jackson, Pamela Irving.
    Minority group threat, crime, and policing : social context and
social control / Pamela Irving Jackson.
      p.   cm.
    Bibliography: p.
    Includes index.
    ISBN 0-275-92983-3 (alk. paper)
    1. Police—United States. 2. Public relations—United States—
Police. 3. United States—Race relations. 4. Minorities—United
States—Social conditions. 5. Social control.   I. Title.
HV8138.J33   1989
363.2'32'0973—dc19   88-31927

Library of Congress Catalog Card Number: 88-31927
ISBN: 0-275-92983-3

First published in 1989

Praeger Publishers, One Madison Avenue, New York, NY 10010
An imprint of Greenwood Publishing Group, Inc.

Printed in the United States of America

The paper used in this book complies with the
Permanent Paper Standard issued by the National
Information Standards Organization (Z39.48-1984).

10 9 8 7 6 5 4 3 2

Contents

Tables and Figures

TABLES

FIGURES

Preface

It is my hope that this book will contribute to our understanding of societal expectations for police work—from national, regional, and local perspectives—and to our recognition of the conflicts within those expectations. We feel the greatest need for policing and we spend the most on law enforcement in those places and periods when we are confronted by social problems and severe intergroup conflict. Yet it is in such situations that policing is least effective and most conflict ridden; social programs and intergroup mediation efforts often prove far more effective, in the long run, in strengthening a community and in reducing crime.

The following pages discuss the challenges and pitfalls facing urban police forces. The evidence presented describes the varying levels of financial support police receive from their communities and details changes in their public image. There are some obvious explanations for the differing levels of fiscal support for city police forces: the size and density of the city population, the city revenue base, and the crime rate, for example. But other explanations for these variations are surprising—differing social contexts in major regions of the United States, in large and small cities, and in different time periods.

The history, traditions, socioeconomic traits, and racial and ethnic population mix of each social context influence the expectations held for police officers: Whether police are expected to be the primary enforcers of law and order or to be "community relations officers"; whether they are expected to use the necessary level of force to establish control, or to avoid physical force whenever possible and refrain from deadly force; whether or not police departments are pressured to recruit a force reflective of the community's racial and ethnic mix.

Public support for social control is also a consequence of the degree of intergroup tension and conflict in a city. Both historical evidence and current cross-cultural investigation suggest that formal social control efforts increase when minority groups become large enough numerically to threaten the majority's economic or political lifestyle.

The central thesis of this book is that when the national emphasis on law and order triggered mobilization of municipal police resources in the early 1970s, the proportion minority in a city influenced the degree of mobilization, especially in areas of historically tense minority/majority relations. The book investigates this thesis through quantitative analysis of the determinants of municipal police force spending in U.S. cities of 25,000 or more population. Comparing beginning and end of the decade determinants in different regions and in large and small cities, the analysis yields some conclusions and provides considerable evidence regarding the mobilization of police resources in periods and locations of intergroup tension and conflict.

Newspaper reporting of the police and issues of police/minority relations in a selected group of the study's cities adds depth to the analysis by providing the public perspective on policing in various locations and time periods. The investigation compares early and late in the decade reporting and assesses changes in perspective as national attention during that time period shifted from law and order and the containment of black unrest to other policy issues and new minorities. The newspaper analysis indicates that during the 1970s, a new awareness of the role of the police developed on the local level. There was a recognition of the stress that officers are under, their lack of training for the major interpersonal crises with which they deal, and the generally inadequate provisions most departments make for stress treatment of officers. An article in the *Miami Herald* (7/25/79b) quoted one counselor's assessment of the situation:

[w]ith a minimum of training in human relations, policemen are called upon to deal with social conflicts at the greatest moment of crisis—conflicts that need extended treatment. . . . The rest of society hasn't been able to provide the services to deal with them. So they feed back on the police.

By the end of the decade, there was a better understanding of how the degree to which police officers provide a buffer between the privileged and the underprivileged in U.S. cities contributes to this stress. There was also a realization of the alienation police officers feel from those they serve—from both the disadvantaged members of the community they come in contact with daily, and the advantaged members of the community who often hold police in low esteem for the company their work requires them to keep.

A 37-year-old Miami police officer put it this way: "We draw the fire. . . . If somebody wants to do something to a symbol of society, here I am. I've got the writing on the side of the car" (*Miami Herald*, 7/25/79b). "Equally demoralizing to an officer's perception," editorialized the *Wichita Eagle* (6/27/79), "is the adage: 'When you spend every day working in the sewer with the scum, it tends to affect your thinking.'"

Even as we reflect on the situation of urban police during the 1970 to 1980 period, we must recognize that it has not improved as we move into the 1990s. During the 1980s older central cities have increasingly lost labor-market opportunities and been left primarily to unskilled minority populations. To maintain stability, police have been called upon in lieu of the social supports once provided by the black middle class and the institutions (such as the church and schools) that were strengthened by their presence (cf. Wilson, 1987). Police cannot meet the expectations we have set for them in decaying inner cities, populated largely by minority group members who constitute an economic underclass (Wilson, 1987; Skolnick and Bayley, 1986); law enforcement officers cannot provide a source of stability where "everything's out of control" (Wichita Police chief La Munyon, *Wichita Eagle,* 6/27/79). And as was recognized in the late 1970s, police cannot effectively reduce crime; only social and economic programs can do that (*Detroit Free Press,* 6/24/79; Heinz et al., 1983: 87).

Impossible expectations have been established for urban police forces. Realistic appraisal of the limits of police work would enable more accurate determination of the situations in which the force can be most highly utilized. Expecting police to be the major source of stability or to provide effective control in communities lacking both economic resources and social integration sets law enforcement officers up for failure, with a resulting increase in their stress levels and the likelihood of their disillusionment with police work. City mayors, as the following pages indicate, have come to understand the limitations of law enforcement; so have many officers themselves. When the general public recognizes these limits, it will be better able to appreciate the strengths of law enforcement, and begin to structure the police officer's role to capitalize on those strengths.

1

Minority Group Threat, Crime, and Policing

In the 1970s, social scientific study of the impact of social context on public support for policing began in earnest with efforts to gauge the influence of urban riots on municipal policing resources. This avenue of investigation signaled revision of the traditional theoretical model guiding criminal justice research on police strength. Until then, social and historical community characteristics—such as the system of stratification and the distribution of power—were seen as relevant to models of police strength only insofar as they were determinants of crime. From this perspective, proper specification of the crime function obviated the need for their inclusion in the policing model; observed associations between minority group presence and police strength were explained as resulting from the higher crime rate in communities with significant minority presence.

This chapter traces the development of a much broader theoretical perspective—a perspective that includes social and historical inequality and discrimination as bases of public support for police resources. The chapter will identify the central concepts of the current perspective and consider conceptual linkages, indicating which have been established by research and which are still in need of research confirmation.

SHIFTS IN THEORETICAL PERSPECTIVES

Early Models

Models of police expenditures in the 1960s, developed largely by economists who argued that a community's "taste" for policing is influenced by the size of the minority groups within it, still specified models in which crime was the major determinant of collective support for policing (cf. G. Becker, 1968).

Earlier models (see Brazer, 1959; Weicher, 1970, for example) had not included crime in the paradigm, and had focused instead on measures of city size, inter-governmental revenues, metropolitan political fragmentation, and fiscal capacity. The newer models included these variables and also assumed reciprocity between the crime rate and police strength: Higher crime rates lead to a buildup of police resources and strengthened police forces reduce crime (for example, McPheters and Stronge, 1974; Greenwood and Wadycki, 1973). For over a decade, the reciprocity assumption influenced policy development and the interpretation of research results.

By the end of the 1970s, criminologists began to question this belief and the research that supported it. Labeling theory (cf. Lemert, 1951; H. Becker, 1963; Schur, 1972; Gove, 1975) had gained sufficient acceptance to give meaning and significance to the inconsistency and paucity of evidence relating to the reciprocity assumption, and criminal justice researchers turned their investigations to the effects of social class, race, and ethnicity. As more sophisticated longitudinal techniques were developed and employed in this area (cf. Greenberg et al., 1983; Loftin and McDowall, 1982), fault was found with assumptions fundamental to the statistical technique (two-stage least-squares regression) used to model the reciprocal relationship between crime and police strength. These new studies provided no evidence to support the deterrent effect of policing on crime, nor did they indicate an immediate short-run effect of crime on policing.

On the basis of such work, Loftin and McDowall (1982: 399) argued that the relationship between crime and police strength is far from direct and immediate. Rather, they said, it is more like "a soft and squishy marshmallow" molded broadly by socially patterned interests and hierarchies in and of themselves, not solely through their impact on the crime rate. Thus, a more complicated sociological theory of collective response to crime evolved. Police strength and the degree of collective fiscal support for policing were seen as responding directly to social system characteristics that had hitherto been viewed as influencing policing resources only through crime (cf. McPheters and Stronge, 1974: 636). The relative economic and political power of a community's racial and ethnic groups, the degree of poverty, and the level of inequality were added to revenues, crime, population size, and density as possible determinants of the collective response to crime.

The Current Model

The relationship between minority group presence and threat and collective support for formal social control activities has emerged as a complicated area of investigation. It has, however, great potential for illuminating our understanding of the social construction of majority/minority group relationships and the salience of crime rates on public behavior. Recent work in this area, published largely during the 1980s, has contributed to development of the model diagrammed in Figure 1.1.

Figure 1.1
Linkage of Racial and Economic Inequality to Social Control
Resource Determination

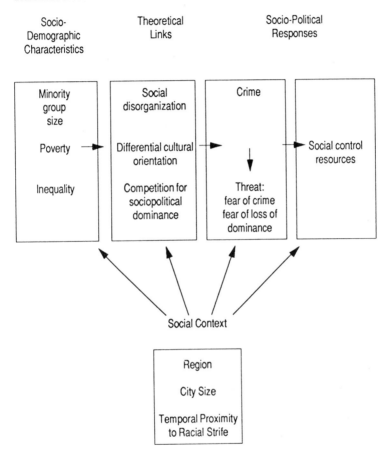

On the left-hand side of the diagram are community characteristics that foster both crime and minority threat. Three middle range sociological theories explain the impact of these sociodemographic characteristics on crime and on social control resources.

1. Social disorganization theory, with its emphasis on the disintegration of informal social control fostered by population heterogeneity, provides one link between the levels of minority group size/poverty/inequality and social control resources by way of the influence of social disorganization on both crime and degree of minority group threat (cf. Shaw and McKay, 1972).

2. Subcultural theory also helps explain the impact of minority group size on social control resources by highlighting the criminogenic and threatening repercussions of

close proximity between groups that have been socialized to different value systems and cultural orientations (cf. Miller, 1958).

3. Conflict theory provides explanatory links between minority group size/poverty/ inequality and social control resources through propositions tying both crime rates and minority group threat to the hierarchical class structures of capitalist societies (cf. Quinney, 1970).

Blalock's (1967) efforts to build a theoretical model of minority/majority group behavior have been instrumental in developing the most recent model's underlying work in this substantive area. Central to Blalock's model is a proposition that relates minority group size and majority group dominance protection efforts. Majority groups, Blalock argued, escalate efforts to protect their dominance at a geometrically increasing rate as the size of the minority group increases until the minority group becomes or exceeds 50 percent of the population of the social unit.

Researchers, focusing on policing as an agency of formal social control, have developed models of the determinants of policing expenditures and police force size and tested for the curvilinearity that Blalock suggests should be characteristic of this relationship (see, for example, Jacobs, 1979; Jackson and Carroll, 1981; Jackson, 1985, 1986). These studies have been based on the work of Blalock and the conflict theorists, who point to the mid-nineteenth century development of the police as a response to the threat posed by the volatile, riotous agglomerations of poor then entering the urban scene. Since poverty and inequality are facets of minority status, their effects on social control resources were also assessed in these studies. The results indicate that minority group presence influences the level of collective fiscal commitment to policing even after controls for crime and other socioeconomic conditions have been effected. This research also generally supports the proposition that economic and political tensions in the minority/majority relationship are reflected in the level of policing expenditures. Overall, then, there is empirical support for the relationship between minority group size, competition for sociopolitical dominance, and the level of policing resources.

Fear of Crime

Additional work by Liska, Lawrence, and Benson (1981) and by Heinz, Jacob, and Lineberry (1983) suggests that whites' fear of crime is greater in the presence of a visible, culturally dissimilar minority group. Liska et al., in a study of 109 large U.S. cities, found that even after controlling for crime and city size, the impact of percent black on municipal police force strength was greatest after the 1960s' civil disorders and in areas with less residential segregation. Thus, these authors argue that whites' perception of the magnitude and seriousness of the crime problem is greater in nonsegregated communities. They support this interpretation through analysis of data for the 26 cities in the National Crime Survey (Law Enforcement Assistance Administration, 1978b), indicating that whites are more likely to be afraid to walk in their neighborhood at night in nonsegregated communities where interracial victimization is more common. Liska, Lawrence, and Benson go on to suggest that "[t]he percentage of nonwhites in a political unit may then directly affect whites' perception of the crime problem, and by influencing the level of inter-racial victimization it may also affect the level of fear which whites associate with victimization" (1981:415).

The influence of minority group presence on the public's perception of crime is complicated largely because it involves several dimensions (cf. Heinz et al., 1983) including degree of concern about the crime issue and personal assessment of the risk of victimization. Concern about crime is greatest among those who also indicate opposition to black economic and social advances and not necessarily among those who assess their risk of victimization to be highest. Personal assessment of victimization risk, on the other hand, is related as expected to neighborhood crime rate and perceived character of the neighborhood. Concern about the crime issue is not related to personal risk assessment, however. So it may be that whites translate their prejudice or unease about race relations into a concern about the crime issue whether or not they feel personality at risk of crime (cf. Heinz et al., 1983: 79).

If this is the case, then interracial tension influences public perception of the crime problem. Inequality between blacks and whites fosters interracial tension both because relative deprivation breeds minority discontent and because whites feel more threatened where the economic position of blacks is not clearly subordinate. Status position anxiety fosters intergroup hostility. The congruence of economic and racial inequality thereby accentuates the likelihood of intergroup conflict (cf. Blau and Blau, 1982) and fosters the implicit competition that is another element of the threat whites feel from minority group members.

Threat

Minority group threat is based on fear of losing dominance to a culturally dissimilar group. It is influenced by minority size because social disorganization, cultural differences, and sociopolitical dominance questions are more pressing where the subordinate group is larger (Skogan and Maxfield, 1981). These factors influence a community's crime rate, increasing both the actual risk of victimization and the level of concern about crime. Such tensions result in greater public support for social control efforts (cf. Heinz et al., 1983) to resolve the dominance question and to control crime.

SOCIAL CONTEXT

The strength of the theoretical links specified in the model varies with a region's social context, city size, and temporal proximity to racial strife. The degree to which each influences public perceptions of crime and minority groups depends on historical and cultural tradition, variations in sociodemographic characteristics, and experience.

Region

Climate, history, tradition, and sociodemographic composition show marked regional variation in the United States. The relationship between these elements and crime rates, which also show persistent regional variation, has been the subject of considerable investigation (see, for example, Brantingham and Brantingham, 1984; Pyle, 1976; Gastil, 1971; Hackney, 1969). While the impact of regional contextual differences on the determinants of public support for policing has not received the same degree of scrutiny, the evidence available suggests that the historical pattern of minority/majority group relations in a region influences the level of fiscal support for policing as well as the degree of attention accorded to the "crime problem" (cf. Jackson, 1985).

City Size

The impact of minority group size on the level of public fiscal commitment to policing has been found to be greater in larger cities (Jackson, 1986). It may be that the anonymity and reduced social control characteristic of large cities increase the public's fear of crime and the degree of threat represented by a minority group. In smaller cities, on the other hand, informal surveillance and greater levels of social cohesion may inhibit crime and reduce the perception of minority group threat to the existing order.

Temporal Proximity to Racial Strife

Recent work supports the view of historical analysts of the police, suggesting the majority group concern with the "dangerous classes" dissipates with declines in rioting and protest activity (cf. Silver, 1967). As noted earlier, Liska, Lawrence, and Benson (1981) found that the impact of the relative size of the black population on the size of municipal police forces was greatest after the civil disorders of the 1960s, even when the level of crime and city population size were controlled. It is likely, then, that researchers will find that minority group size had a greater impact on public fiscal commitment to policing earlier in the 1970s, just after the period of urban racial strife, than it did in the later 1970s when minority/majority conflicts had subsided.

POLICING AND POLITICS

It is difficult for police or other public officials to keep politics out of the funding process because budget determination is a public process. Policing and other emergency services are extremely labor intensive and undercapitalized. Employee salaries and fringe benefits account for more than 90 percent of the budget in most cities, while the patrol force accounts for almost half of the total police budget. Patrol units spend more than fifty percent of their time in preventive patrol (cf. Larson, 1972: 1-10)—removing crime hazards and providing a threat of apprehension by their presence.

Although preventive patrol is central to municipal law enforcement programs, "no widely accepted methods are employed for determining the need for patrol" (Larson, 1972: 131). The dearth of knowledge regarding the resources and methods necessary to accomplish this central police function has been obvious for some time (cf. President's Commission on Law Enforcement and Administration of Justice, 1967). There is little solid information on the service improvement and crime reduction impact of specific patterns of deployment and types of patrol activity. The hazard and workload formulas developed in the 1930s (cf. O. W. Wilson, 1941, 1972) use a weighted set of statistics—number of reported and attempted crimes, number of arrests, number of radio calls, amount of property loss, police services rendered, population size and density, road miles, licensed premises, store doors, and schools—to predict the size and location of the patrol force. They yield no information, however, about the response time of the patrol force or the probability that a crime will be intercepted in progress. As a result, the deployment of municipal patrol units is determined largely on the basis of the judgment and intuition that commanding officers have acquired during their years of police work (cf. Larson, 1972: 6, 150).

In the absence of hard evidence on the deterrent capacity of specific deployment levels or patterns, and despite the fact that official police funding requests may be based on sound professional judgment, police department reliance on city appropriations allows politics to influence overall police funding levels. Investigations of the sociopolitical influences on public fiscal commitment to policing indicate three categories of determinants:

1. *The community's need for policing: crime rate, population size, and density.* Cities with large populations and high densities increase the ease of crime commission and exacerbate the problems of policing. It is no surprise that large, densely populated cities spend more per capita for policing than less populated communities. First, traffic control and service-related problems are more difficult in highly populated environments. Second, the heterogeneity and anonymity characteristic of these communities reduce the ability of social cohesion and informal surveillance to provide a sufficient level of informal social control to deter crime. In addition, as population size and density increase, so do the number of criminal opportunities and targets.

The officially acknowledged rate of crime may also influence public willingness to pay for policing despite the fact that neither social scientists nor the public can be sure "about the exact point where additional policemen are no longer worth their additional cost . . . " (Jacobs, 1979: 921).

2. *The community's ability to appropriate funds for policing: revenues and poverty.* Municipal fiscal capacity has some important and obvious links to public fiscal commitment to policing because the city revenue base is the primary source for all categories of expenditures. It has become apparent, however, that in the absence of severe limitations of resources, policing takes

precedence over other areas of municipal spending, especially where fear of crime is high (cf. Heinz et al., 1983).

Relatively large poor populations reduce the municipal revenue base and thereby restrict the community's ability to pay for policing and other municipal services, giving rise to the proposition that policing may be neglected (relatively speaking) in large, poor communities. However, it has also been suggested that since the poor rely on the police as service providers more often than more affluent groups, cities with large poor populations may require greater expenditures on policing than cities with smaller poor populations. Percent poor can be viewed, then, both as an indicator of the community's ability to pay for policing and as a measure of its need for police provided services.

3. *Minority group threat: minority size and economic subordinance.* The recent studies noted above suggest that minority group presence influences the level of collective fiscal commitment to policing even after controls for crime and other socioeconomic conditions have been effected, and that economic and political tensions in the minority/majority group relationship are reflected in the level of policing expenditures. More research is needed, however, to augment our understanding of the operation of these political processes on police budget setting.

THEORETICAL IMPLICATIONS

As it is impossible to determine objectively the exact level of police financing required to control crime in a given set of circumstances, public fiscal commitment to policing—like other areas of societal resource commitment—can be influenced by elements of stratification and power. There is some evidence, for example, that a national trend toward arming municipal police departments in the early 1970s was facilitated by the Law Enforcement Assistance Administration's (LEAA) efforts to equip and train police officers to deal effectively with riots (cf. Feeley and Sarat, 1980; Michalowski, 1985).

In considering the effects of the turbulence of the 1960s, Feagin and Hahn (1973), Button (1978), and others have argued that the Justice Department's response was more forceful than any other branch of the federal government's, and that this response had serious consequences for municipal police activity. It is possible that the federal war on crime and the general law and order reaction to the disturbances of the 1960s stimulated and financially supported the reinforcement of hostile police-community relations where they already existed, and encouraged the development of such an atmosphere where they did not. In a sample of 40 riot cities, Button found that the cities with the worst minority-police relations used LEAA funds to stock up on hardware. The availability of funds for protective hardware and intelligence devices might have encouraged other police departments to purchase them as well. Once owned, this equipment may have prompted the development of proactive (cf. Reiss and Bordua, 1967: 25-66) or even repressive police work.

Since recent analyses demonstrate that the level of early 1970s' police expenditures (especially capital police expenditures) responded to the relative size of the minority population and its level of political mobilization activity (Jackson and Carroll, 1981), it is possible that the political solidarity and activity of blacks in the late 1960s and of Hispanic ethnic groups in the early 1970s may have cost them as much in terms of their civil rights as they gained.

FUTURE RESEARCH DIRECTIONS

Study of public resource commitment to policing has broadened in perspective during the past 20 years. Poverty, inequality, and minority group size, once considered to be related to policing expenditures only insofar as they influenced the rate of crime, are now seen to be important in police resource determination. Although the impact of stratification and power on public commitment to social control has been established, the exact nature of the links of minority group size, poverty, inequality, crime, and threat with social control resource determination has not yet been specified and requires more theoretical and empirical consideration. Areas to be further researched involve the extent to which stratification, the distribution of power, and minority group threat (a) influence the political processes determining the size of a community's policing budget, and (b) affect the nature and quality of policing activity, the hostility level of police/community relations, and the direction of municipal policing funds toward development of a weapons arsenal and training in crowd and riot control.

Some of these areas are closely related to each other. Minority group threat, for example, is integrally related to patterns of stratification and power distribution. But since the overlapping of racial and economic heterogeneity represents a distinct and severe form of stratification and inequality (cf. Blau and Blau, 1982), the threat generated by minority group presence merits study separate from the general patterns and consequences of stratification.

On the basis of a national analysis, the succeeding pages provide research in these areas and further examine the social control consequences of stratification and minority/majority conflict to shed additional light on policing. Throughout the discussion care is taken to separate issues related to the politics of funding from those relating to patterns of police behavior.

Overall Plan

The following chapters discuss the findings of a national cross-sectional analysis of the determinants of public fiscal commitment to policing in U.S. cities of 25,000 or more during the 1970s. The implications of the analysis for the links among minority group threat, crime, and policing are drawn out. Illustrative case studies are presented throughout to clarify the discussion and to add depth to the results of the national quantitative analysis.

Chapter 2 provides an overview of the study's data, methods, and theoretical significance. Chapter 3 begins presentation of the national evidence on the relationship between minority visibility and the mobilization of social control resources and details the influence of city size as an important contextual demarcator. Chapter 4 investigates the influence of region as a sociohistorical construct on the strength of the police resource/social control allocation relationship. Chapter 5 clarifies changes in the strength of this relationship and in the relative impact of black and Hispanic visibility on police resource allocation between 1971 and 1978 in large industrial cities. Change during the decade is detailed for mid-sized cities in Chapter 6, and for southern and western cities in Chapter 7. Finally, in Chapter 8, the results of the national and case study analyses are reviewed, distilled, and integrated into a summary of existing knowledge in the field, paving the way for future research efforts.

2

Social Context in National and Historical Perspective

Policing, crime, and minority group threat reflect the constellation of individuals and social conditions present in a community. Demographic and socioeconomic community traits are included in the model of collective support for policing. These characteristics alone, however, do not reveal the long-term intergroup animosities characteristic of a region or a specific time period; nor do they capture the relatively greater anonymity and social isolation of larger cities. These and other attributes of clearly defined social contexts are expected to influence a city's response to a visible minority presence in the community, and to affect the level of a city's expenditures for police.

Regional subpopulations of cities differ from each other not only in demographic and economic traits, but also in the historical context within which funding decisions are made. In the Southwest, for example, persistent tension between Anglos and Hispanics may influence the degree of threat triggered by the presence of a large Hispanic population, while in the South, the history of conflict between blacks and whites can be expected to influence the extent to which blacks are perceived as threatening. Similarly, the passage of time and events affect the social and economic expectations of minority and majority individuals, thereby influencing their patterns of behavior and the level of intergroup hostility. In addition, city size influences the nature of the bonds between individuals, and thus the degree to which informal social mechanisms succeed in regulating relationships among individuals and groups. Variations in the determinants of municipal funding for law enforcement may reflect contextual differences in the level of intergroup fear and hostility and in the perception of how important policing is in both crime control and the preservation of traditional patterns of order.

CONTEXTUAL VARIATIONS

The urban profiles presented in this chapter depict some objective differences between large and small cities, regional groupings of cities, and groupings based on special combinations of region and size with temporal comparisons throughout. Although discussed briefly here, these objective characteristics are relatively unimportant in and of themselves; it is their social significance that is important in any effort to understand variations in public support for collective social control. After consideration of the data and methods of investigation, the implications of the contextual distinctions are analyzed.

The Data

This study is based on data for all U.S. cities of 25,000 or more population. Information for two points in time—one at or near 1970, the other at or near 1980—was obtained from the Law Enforcement Assistance Administration (1971, 1978a) and the U.S. Bureau of the Census (1970, 1980). Summary data for the population groupings of the study are presented in Tables 2.1-2.7 and in Tables A.1 and A.7.

Table 2.1
Urban Profile: All Cities ≥ 25,000 Population

Characteristic	1970	1980
Number of Cities	442	569*
Average Size	152 thsnd	131 thsnd
Average Variation in Size	456 thsnd	369 thsnd
Population Density	4800 sqmi	4300 sqmi
Per Capita Revenue	$181	$528
Per Cent Poor	10%	10%
Per Cent Black	14%	15%
Per Cent Hispanic	7%	8%
Black/White Median Income	.68	.72
Crime Rate Per Thousand	31	80
Police Expenditures		
Total	$24	$45
Salaries/Operations	$24	$43
Capital	$1	$2

*For all seven Urban Profiles, 1980 comparisons using only the 442 cities for which 1970 data were available indicate no noteworthy differences in the figures.

Table 2.2
Urban Profile: Cities ≥ 50,000 Population

Characteristic	1970	1980
Number of Cities	281	378
Average Size	219 thsnd	178 thsnd
Average Variation in Size	562 thsnd	445 thsnd
Population Density	5300 sqmi	4700 sqmi
Per Capita Revenue	$195	$559
Per Cent Poor	10%	10%
Per Cent Black	15%	14%
Black/White Median Income	.67	.72
Crime Rate Per Thousand	34	81
Police Expenditures		
Total	$27	$48
Salaries/Operations	$25	$46
Capital	$1	$2.3

Table 2.3
Urban Profile: Cities of 25,000-50,000 Population

Characteristic	1970	1980
Number of Cities	161	191
Average Size	36 thsnd	37 thsnd
Average Variation in Size	7 thsnd	7 thsnd
Population Density	4000 sqmi	3400 sqmi
Per Capita Revenue	$157	$467
Per Cent Poor	10%	11%
Per Cent Black	12%	18%
Black/White Median Income	.68	.70
Crime Rate Per Thousand	27	78
Police Expenditures		
Total	$21	$39
Salaries/Operations	$20	$37
Capital	$.7	$1.3

Table 2.4
Urban Profile: Southern and Western Cities

Characteristic	1970	1980
Number of Cities	175	302
Average Size	161 thsnd	126 thsnd
Average Variation in Size	264 thsnd	218 thsnd
Population Density	3500 sqmi	3500 sqmi
Per Capita Revenue	$156	$481
Per Cent Poor	11%	11%
Per Cent Black	15%	17%
Per Cent Hispanic	10%	12%
Black/White Median Income	.64	.68
Crime Rate Per Thousand	36	85
Police Expenditures		
Total	$24	$43
Salaries/Operations	$23	$41
Capital	$1	$2

Table 2.5
Urban Profile: Northeastern and North Central Cities

Characteristic	1970	1980
Number of Cities	142	267
Average Size	231 thsnd	136 thsnd
Average Variation in Size	740 thsnd	486 thsnd
Population Density	6600 sqmi	5100 sqmi
Per Capita Revenue	$223	$582
Per Cent Poor	11%	11%
Per Cent Black	13%	14%
Per Cent Hispanic	3%	4%
Black/White Median Income	.72	.76
Crime Rate Per Thousand	33	75
Police Expenditures		
Total	$28	$48
Salaries/Operations	$27	$46
Capital	$1	$2

Table 2.6
Urban Profile: Southern Cities ≥ 50,000 Population

Characteristic	1970	1980
Number of Cities	84	99
Average Size	171 thsnd	169 thsnd
Average Variation in Size	176 thsnd	172 thsnd
Population Density	3100 sqmi	2900 sqmi
Per Capita Revenue	$163	$573
Per Cent Poor	14%	13%
Per Cent Black	23%	25%
Black/White Median Income	.55	.61
Crime Rate Per Thousand	33	88
Police Expenditures		
Total	$21	$44
Salaries/Operations	$20	$42
Capital	$1	$2

Table 2.7
Urban Profile: Southern Cities of 25,000-50,000 Population

Characteristic	1970	1980
Number of Cities	52	68
Average Size	35 thsnd	38 thsnd
Average Variation in Size	7 thsnd	7 thsnd
Population Density	2700 sqmi	2300 sqmi
Per Capita Revenue	$133	$459
Per Cent Poor	15%	14%
Per Cent Black	20%	25%
Black/White Median Income	.56	.58
Crime Rate Per Thousand	25	81
Police Expenditures		
Total	$18	$34
Salaries/Operations	$17	$32
Capital	$1	$1

Each city's municipal fiscal commitment to policing is reflected by three measures: reported expenditures for police salaries and operations, capital police expenditures, and the sum of the two.[1] Data on these variables for 1971 and 1978, originally gathered and published by the Law Enforcement Assistance Administration (1971, 1978a), were provided by the Criminal Justice Archive Information Network (CJAIN). Since national funding for municipal police activities began in a significant way in 1971, slowing to a trickle by the mid-1970s (cf. Button, 1978; Community Relations Service, 1973, 1974), it is expected that these time periods will reflect both federal and municipal shifts in law and order priorities (cf. Skolnick and Bayley, 1986).

The city characteristics expected to influence police spending levels are the total crime rate, obtained from the Federal Bureau of Investigation's Uniform Crime Reports for 1970 and 1980, measured as the sum of the Part I Index Offenses (excluding arson); and city revenues, crime, population size, density, interracial inequality, percent black and percent Hispanic, as reported in the 1970 and 1980 U.S. Census. These variables have been increasingly included in studies of police force size and expenditures as the importance of inequality and race/ethnic relations in determining public commitment to social control has been recognized (cf. Brazer, 1959; G. Becker, 1968; Weicher, 1970; Greenwood and Wadycki, 1973; Jacobs, 1979; Jackson and Carroll, 1981; Liska et al., 1981; Loftin and McDowell, 1982; Greenberg et al., 1983).

Method

To demonstrate the influence of regional location on the strength and form of the impact of minority visibility on social control efforts, the analysis is replicated within, and compared across regions. Because city size has been implicated as an important contextual demarcator, it too provides a basis of comparison. Throughout this study two time periods are compared—one early, the other late in the 1970s—to assess any changes in the form or strength of the minority visibility/social control relationship during the decade. Since the racially quiescent 1970s were also a period of rapid migration of Hispanic population groups into U.S. cities, municipal fiscal allocations for social control were expected to be influenced decreasingly by the size of the black population and increasingly by the size of Hispanic ethnic groups during this period, following the direction of national government priorities (cf. Button, 1978).

National Analysis

Ordinary least-squares regression was used to estimate the determinants of public fiscal commitment to policing and to compare the degree of influence exerted by individual variables when others are controlled. The results are discussed in the following chapters and presented in tabular form in the Appendix.[2]

By repeating the analysis within specific regions, city size groupings, and time periods, the influence of social context on the configuration of determinants of public fiscal commitment to policing is assessed. Context is expected to influence the visibility of blacks and Hispanics, the threat posed by them, and the impact of other variables on policing expenditures. While the individual effect of each contextual variable could be assessed by including it in dummy variable form within the regression analysis, the influence of context on the interactions among the independent variables and therefore ultimately on their impact on policing expenditures would not be provided for by this technique. Repetition of the analysis for groupings of cities that share a given context will provide for assessment of the influences of common contextual understandings on the relationships among minority group threat, crime, and policing expenditures.

Case Study Analysis

Throughout the book detailed consideration of some cities is undertaken with a view toward mapping out the interactions between community structure and collective fiscal support for policing. The characteristics of each city's sociodemographic structure and police expenditure levels are considered, as is the newspaper reading public's view of police/community tensions and police resource mobilization during the 1970s.[3] For a group of 14 intensively investigated cities, discussion centers on the changes in 1970 to 1980 demographic characteristics, growth in the level of policing expenditures from early to late in the decade, and newspaper accounts of police funding priorities and issues relating to police/community relations.

The newspaper review covers 1972, since 1971 policing expenditures, programs, and capital purchases are expected to influence the issues of the next year, and because other research on the contextual importance of the temporal proximity to racial strife suggests that police-related reporting early in the decade will reflect the links between minority group threat, crime and policing. There is also some follow-up attention to 1979 to 1980 reporting as a sequel to 1978 expenditure levels. Two major categories of reported issues are reviewed: (1) issues relating to expenditures (for example, the source of major grants for policing and the items subsequently purchased), and (2) issues relating to police/community relations, including allegations of brutality and efforts to recruit more minority group members on the police force.

One premise of this portion of the investigation is that items reported in the newspaper have become a part of the public agenda. Newspaper accounts often contain some erroneous elements. While the actual facts of the story sometimes become evident in successive reporting on the event, errors of fact and interpretation influence public perceptions when reported in the newspaper and reviewed by readers. There may be better ways to find the facts, but analysis of newspaper reporting on a topic provides a good barometer of the issues on the public's mind.

Differences between Contextual Divisions

Large versus Small Cities

As expected, all categories of policing expenditures are greater in the large cities than in the subgroup of small cities. Several obvious differences in the policing needs of each group made this difference predictable: Traffic control and other service-related problems place greater demands on law enforcement agencies in large cities (cf. Brazer, 1959; Weicher, 1970; Rubinstein, 1973), and large cities have higher crime rates than small cities (cf. Harries, 1974; Pyle, 1976).

Other important differences between the two groups, consequences of their objective characteristics, are less obvious. For example, large, densely populated cities have greater levels of anonymity and more heterogeneity, lower levels of social cohesion, and less informal surveillance than small cities (cf. Fischer, 1984: 139-141; Liska et al., 1981; Wirth, 1938). These characteristics all handicap policing activity (cf. Ogburn, 1935; Pyle, 1976; Harries, 1974; Wolfgang, 1968; Blau and Blau, 1982; Mayhew and Levinger, 1976; Jacobs, 1982). In addition, the fiscal capacity of large cities is subjected to greater service provision strains (for policing, fire, education, and other social services), making it more difficult for large cities to appropriate funds for policing.

Fear of crime may be greater in large cities, partly because the actual rate of crime is higher, and partly because the greater levels of anonymity and heterogeneity and the lower levels of social cohesion and informal social control, characteristic of large cities, exacerbate fear of crime beyond the level produced by the actual likelihood of crime (cf. Fischer, 1984: 108). Because of the relationships hypothesized in Figure 1.1, it is likely that these characteristics of larger cities intensify the effect of minority size on collective fiscal support for social control; this was especially evident in 1971, right after the racial disturbances of the 1960s.

Region

The higher overall crime rates in the southern and the southern/western groups of cities (seen in Tables 2.4 through 2.7) are not surprising in light of the literature depicting stable historical regional variations in crime (cf. Brantingham and Brantingham, 1984; Pyle, 1976; Harries, 1971, 1974; Kowalski et al., 1980). (See Appendix Tables A.1 and A.7 for comparative purposes.) Viewed as a cultural phenomenon by some, and a result of sociodemographic patterns by others, these patterns have been the subject of a long, sometimes bitter debate (see, for example, Gastil, 1971; Hackney, 1969; Loftin and Hill, 1974).

Recent efforts have focused on assessing variations in the regional determinants of crime (cf. Messner, 1983), and take into account regional variations in the lifestyle of urban inhabitants, opportunity factors, target vulnerability, and guardianship (cf. Reppetto, 1974; Boggs, 1965; Cohen and Felson, 1979). Work in this area is beginning to suggest that crime is an unintended consequence of affluence, the anonymity bred by mobility and large city size, and family lifestyles that leave dwellings empty, possessions unguarded, and put people in transit—where they can be personally victimized (cf. Mansfield, Gould, and Namenwirth, 1974; Jackson, 1984). It is possible that the convergence of likely offenders, suitable targets, and absent guardians may vary by region. Regional variations in climate, culture (cf. Zelinsky, 1973), and the nature and abundance of economic opportunities influence the recreational and occupational lifestyle of households, a community's migration patterns, and the pervasiveness of opportunities for legitimate success.

Regional context has important implications for several other elements in the model, most notably the degree of minority/majority competition for sociopolitical dominance and the degree of minority group threat. Tables 2.4-2.7 indicate persistent regional variations in the size of minority populations, with a greater percentage of blacks in southern cities and a larger percentage of Hispanic ethnic group members in cities of the South and West. Intergroup conflict has been most persistent in the South and Southwest, as have the problems of poverty and interracial income inequality.

1970 versus 1980

The total population of cities changed between 1970 and 1980. The average size of cities declined during the decade as did population density. This decline is evident in all but the small cities (25,000-50,000); they increased slightly in size.[4] The decline in the attractiveness of major cities for residential and business purposes and the out-migration of businesses and workers to less congested locations are reflected in these figures. The level of poverty in the total, large, and small city groups did not differ much between 1970 and 1980. Comparison of the ratio of black to white median income indicates that there was, on average, less inequality in urban centers in 1980, when the value was about 0.72, than in 1970, when the average value was about 0.68. Later, discussion and data will provide evidence of a reverse trend—a worsening of blacks' economic situation vis-à-vis whites—in large industrial centers.

The crime rate by 1980 (about 80 per thousand) was over two and one-half times the 1970 level (31 per thousand), a highly publicized fact that may have contributed to the public's fear of crime and willingness to appropriate funds for social control. In addition, the size of the minority population increased slightly, from 14 percent to 15 percent for blacks overall, and from 7 percent to 8 percent for Hispanics. In smaller cities, the size of the black population increased from 12 percent to 18 percent during the decade (see Table 2.3). And as expected, police expenditures were greater for all groups in 1980 than in 1970.

COMMUNITY PERCEPTIONS OF THE POLICE

The image of the police presented to the newspaper reading public in some cities is clarified in the case study analyses. This material provides additional information about the links between the presence of a minority group and the nature of policing.

Police/community relations are fraught with problems of authority and class. Since policing is a tangible manifestation of authority, it taps the pool of resentment in those without resources. As the police are the glue that holds society together when the pervasive moral assent begins to crack, policing interacts with existing social tensions. Although development of the modern police force represented a separation of constitutional authority from social and economic dominance, subordinate groups still view the police as a repressive tool of the dominant group. As a consequence, policing often triggers the unleashing of hostility and violence.

The importance of community perceptions of the police cannot be understimated. In a study of the 1960s U.S. riots, the Kerner Commission documented several instances where police-related incidents ignited riots. The May 1980 riot in Miami has been traced to the acquittal of four policemen accused of beating a black businessman to death. In Liverpool, England, July 1981 rioting in the heavily black Toxteth section began when police searching for a stolen car were attacked by a gang of teenagers wielding stones and bottles (*Time*, July 20, 1981: 30-31). There have been numerous instances of police/community tension triggering riots and violence. As research has shown (cf. Button, 1978; Michalowski, 1985; Liska et al., 1981; Jackson and Carroll, 1981; Carroll and Jackson, 1983), such tensions also lead to the escalation of policing resources.

Analysis of community perceptions of the police will focus on the 14 cities in Table 2.8. The cities, listed in order of their discussion in the following chapters, were selected for in-depth study as examples of a cross-section of urban centers possessing the characteristics that investigation of the overall population suggested were influences on the relationships among minority group threat/crime/and policing. Thus, the group includes cities from all regions and the cities vary in population size and in the size and relative predominance of their black and Hispanic population groups.[5]

The tone of newspaper reporting in each city will be described. Incidents that receive significant coverage will be presented in detail as indicators of the view of the police that is presented to the public. It may be that a city's structural characteristics or the level or pattern of its policing expenditures are in some ways related to the public view that emerges.

Chapter 3 begins discussion of the national evidence relating to minority group presence and public fiscal commitment to social control with special attention to the differences in the strength and form of the relationship in large versus small cities. In-depth investigation of seven of the study cities will provide evidence

Table 2.8
Cities in Community Perceptions of Police Subpopulation

Characteristics

City	Population thousands		% Black		% Hispanic		Crime Rate per thsnd		Police $ per capita Sal/Op		Capital	
	'70	'80	'70	'80	'70	'80	'70	'80	'71	'78	'71	'78
Detroit	1511	1203	44	63	2	2	84	106	53	126	1.2	3.7
Philadelphia	1950	1688	34	38	1	4	23	60	58	188	2.2	1.9
Baltimore	906	787	46	55	1	1	69	97	58	89	.9	.7
Chicago	3367	3005	33	40	7	14	38	65	61	112	1.4	1.1
Newark	382	329	54	58	7	19	83	129	63	99	1.2	1.3
Minneapolis	434	371	4	8	1	1	54	97	26	65	.2	.1
Wichita	277	279	10	11	2	3	40	88	16	35	.3	.5
Miami	335	347	23	25	45	56	71	151	30	60	1.4	.4
Atlanta	495	425	51	67	1	1	55	140	29	64	3.5	2.5
Tulsa	330	361	10	12	1	2	38	89	14	38	.3	1.4
Albuquerque	244	332	2	2	35	34	55	88	22	41	6.5	4.0
Denver	515	492	9	12	17	19	74	119	28	81	1.0	11.0
Sacramento	257	276	11	13	13	14	46	126	35	64	1.0	.2
San Francisco	716	679	13	13	14	12	80	104	51	83	1.0	2.0

concerning police/community relations in cities that are typical and deviant in terms of the relationship between minority size and municipal fiscal support for policing in the national population.

NOTES

1. These data were reported to the Law Enforcement Assistance Administration by city police officials. They do not include expenditures for pension and health plans and other employee benefits since those are often subsidized and regulated by state policy, making interstate comparison of the level of municipal commitment to policing difficult. The data are best used in the aggregate analyses assessing the determinants of municipal fiscal commitment to policing. The large number of cities in the study (566) makes it likely that there are occasional reporting errors for individual cities, but there is no reason to suspect systematic reporting bias.

2. As noted earlier, some multivariate analyses of policing expenditures incorporating crime as an independent variable have used techniques that allow for the assumption that crime and police expenditures are reciprocally related, that is, that higher crime rates produce greater public fiscal commitment to policing which in turn reduces the crime rate.

Tests of the assumption of simultaneity—including a multiwave panel analysis (Greenberg et al., 1983) based on all cities of 50,000 or more in 1960, and a time series analysis within Detroit from 1926 to 1977 (Loftin and McDowell, 1982)—provide no support for it. Therefore, there was no reason to complicate the analysis with two-stage least-squares analysis and its theoretically problematic assumptions (cf. Greenberg, 1979; Jackson, 1985, 1986).

3. *Newsbank,* a reference that classifies and microfilms newspaper articles in 100 U.S. cities, was invaluable in the newspaper review.

4. The decline in mean population size is confined to the large city group (cities greater than or equal to 50,000 population). It appears to reflect a general reduction in the average size of large cities rather than the increase in the number of cities in the group, since population size in 1980 is also lower for the 442 cities of the 1970 analysis. Population density shows a similar pattern.

5. It was not possible to include any of the cities under 25,000 population in this part of the analysis because microfilmed newspaper sources were not readily available for the small city subpopulation.

3

Minority Visibility and Social Control

One result of the racial turbulence of the 1960s was skyrocketing policing costs. The decline of the "pervasive moral assent" that Silver (1967: 12-15) describes as critical for effective policing is partly responsible. As actual or perceived adherence to the central values of the society declines, policing becomes more costly. In a climate of racial and ethnic unrest, minority groups, if a significant proportion of the city population, may be perceived as a threat to conventional values. Thus, their presence may increase fiscal allocations for policing.

Conflict theorists point to the mid-nineteenth century development of the police in response to the threat to the social order posed by the volatile, riotous agglomerations of urban poor—the dangerous classes—that had recently converged on cities. While riots and mobs had historically served to articulate the dissatisfaction of the masses to an elite who offered them at least a grudging response, the urban poor of the mid-nineteenth century, unlike riotous mobs before them, "challenge[d] the fundamentals of the current system" (Silver, 1967: 16) and thereby prompted a permanent, bureaucratic, and institutionalized response that was designed to maintain the existing order.

Alan Silver (1967: 20) notes that in highly specialized and bureaucratized society, "the demand for law and order becomes what it was not before—a constitutional imperative stemming from an unprecedentedly pervasive consensus . . . personified and enforced by police." Protest, riots, and criminality by the urban poor—especially the culturally dissimilar minority group members of the poor—take on a new significance when the image of a pervasively calm society is accepted as ideal. They are viewed as worse than undesirable—as "threatening to the very fabric of social life" (Silver, 1967: 21).

From the perspective of the conflict tradition within sociology, the evolution of a formal legal system is a response to threats to established patterns of authority, power, and economic dominance. In Seagle's (1946: 36) words, "the criminal law springs into life in every great period of class conflict. . . . Law has its origin in the pathology of social relations and functions only when there are frequent disturbances of the social equilibrium." Diamond (1973: 339) concurs and notes that "law arises in the breach of a prior customary order and increases in force with the conflicts that divide political societies internally and among themselves."

Both structural functional and conflict theorists agree that the need or desire for norm-enforcement is one reason for the development of municipal police departments. This trend has been documented cross-nationally and historically. The critical point of division between the two perspectives lies in the delineation of the source of the norms that are enforced. To structural functionalists, the norms being enforced have been deduced from the central values of the society, are ensconced within the legal institution, and permit society to "function in an orderly manner" (Bohannan, 1973: 310). Conflict theorists, on the other hand, argue that in providing for the enforcement of norms, policing maintains the social and economic dominance of some groups at the expense of others.

MINORITY GROUP PRESENCE, FEAR OF CRIME, AND CRIME CONTROL

Even conflict theorists agree that elite concern with the dangerous classes dissipates as riots and protests diminish, and is replaced by concern over criminality in general. However, concern over criminality appears to be related to the racial and ethnic composition of a community. Recent evidence indicates that whites' fear of crime is related to the presence and visibility of a culturally dissimilar minority group (cf. Garofalo, 1979; Liska, Lawrence, and Benson, 1981; Liska, Lawrence, and Sanchirico, 1982; Liska and Baccaglini, 1983; Heinz et al., 1983).

Since public definition of "the crime problem" and public perception of the threat of crime have been found to be associated with the presence of structurally disadvantaged groups in the population (Turk, 1969; Lizotte and Bordua, 1980; Liska, Chamlin, and Reed, 1985), it is not surprising that variations in arrest rates and in the certainty of arrest appear to be affected by the proportion of nonwhites and the level of income inequality in the city population (Liska and Chamlin, 1984; Liska, Chamlin, and Reed, 1985). For street crime, the size of the threatening population appears to influence both the strength of crime control forces and the likelihood of a crime's punishment. However, the influence of percent nonwhite on the arrest rate is direct; it is not mediated through police force size (Liska and Chamlin, 1984: 389).

Although these studies indicate that the arrest rate of nonwhites is higher than that of whites, the nonwhite arrest rate does not vary positively with their proportion in the population. In fact, larger proportions of nonwhites reduce their arrest rate, possibly because the authorities are "insensitive to their legitimate needs for protection from crime" (Liska, 1987: 82). But, in Liska and Chamlin's (1984: 396) words, "because nonwhite arrest rates are so much higher than white arrest rates . . . an increase in the percentage of nonwhites increases the total arrest rate, even though it actually substantially decreases the nonwhite arrest rate."

Available evidence also indicates that residential segregation of nonwhites reduces the influence of percent nonwhite on the overall arrest rate, probably because segregation, like percent nonwhite, increases the level of intra- as opposed to interracial crime. Segregation thereby reduces whites' pressure on authorities to police the minority population, since it is the level of interracial crime that triggers greatest pressure on crime control forces to bolster social control efforts (Liska and Chamlin, 1984; Liska, Chamlin and Reed, 1985).

City Level Determination of Police Service Delivery Patterns

Since studies of police force strength and activity have indicated the influence of the socioeconomic characteristics of the population, Slovak (1987) speculated in a recent study that police service delivery would be influenced by neighborhood-level socioeconomic characteristics. However, that proposition was not supported by the evidence. While the neighborhoods in his study differed from each other socioeconomically and attitudinally, police service delivery style within them did not present sharp, consistent contrasts by neighborhood type. Low income, minority neighborhoods did not have more intrusive (cf. Wilson's typology, 1968) police activity; instead neighborhood patterns of police patrol delivery appear to be set at the city level, as has been found to be characteristic of other neighborhood-level phenomena (cf. Jackson, 1978). Despite the fact that the specific situational aspects of each incident, including the race and economic background of the victim and assailant and the type of crime, affect police behavior, the pattern of police deployment and the amicability of police/minority relations may be determined largely by city, regional, and national influences.

CITY SIZE

Sociological theory in the consensus tradition emphasizes the importance of normative or voluntary processes in maintaining the social order. Law emerges when traditions and fashions, or norms and customs, are no longer sufficient to regulate the pattern of relationships and obligations among individuals and organizations. Increases in the scale and complexity of society that are mirrored in the size and density of population aggregates in local political subdivisions—towns and cities—reduce the ability of norms and custom to regulate the "ought" elements of human and institutional interrelationships. While the customs of all societies "exhibit most of the stigmata cited by any definition of law" (Bohannan, 1973: 308), the increases in the level of anonymity, the reductions in the level of social cohesion, the increase in the pace of change brought about by technology and the functional specialization of society reduce the effectiveness of these informal techniques of social control. Formal law, and hence formal enforcement of the law, evolve as a way out of this dilemma to clarify relationships and obligations.

These understandings suggest that the relative size of the black community has greater influence on the level of policing expenditures in large cities than in small cities, even after controls for other sociodemographic determinants of expenditures. The rationale behind this expectation is that fear of crime and the degree of threat represented by a minority group are not as great in small cities because there is less anonymity and greater reliance on informal social control. The higher levels of social cohesion and informal surveillance in smaller cities may create a context in which blacks appear less visible than they do in large cities.

The influence of city size as a contextual determinant of the impact of minority group threat on the mobilization of policing resources has not received serious scrutiny until recently. Even now, most studies of the relationship between racial composition and level of commitment to social control are based on analysis of large cities (50,000 or more in population) (cf. Jackson and Carroll, 1981; Liska et al., 1981) or Standard Metropolitan Statistical Areas (SMSAs) (cf. Jacobs, 1979).[1]

RESULTS OF THE NATIONAL STUDY

The national study of the determinants of public fiscal commitment to policing in U.S. cities provides some support for conflict theorists' allegation that mobilization of police resources is in part a response to the presence of a visible minority group, and for the proposition that city population size intensifies the link between the relative size of the minority population and the social control response. (The data are contained in Tables A.2, A.3, and A.4 and are summarized in Tables 3.1-3.4.)

In large cities (50,000 or more population) the statistically significant predictors of 1971 total police expenditures were, in order of explanatory importance, the crime rate, per capita city revenue, percent poor, population density, percent black, and population size (see Table 3.1). Over two-thirds (70 percent) of the variance in total expenditures was explained by the determinants in the model. The results were similar for 1971 salaries and operations.

The Threat Curve

The non-linear model provides the best fit for the 1971 capital expenditures equation, as it increases the explained variance from 21 percent to 22 percent (a statistically significant hike). (See Table 3.2.) The pattern of this curve suggests

Table 3.1
**Significant Predictors of Total Municipal Police Expenditures,
Cities ≥ 50,000 Population, 1971**

```
CITY CRIME RATE      (+)

CITY REVENUES        (+)

PER CENT POOR        (-)

POPULATION DENSITY   (+)

PERCENT BLACK        (+)

POPULATION SIZE      (+)
```

```
EXPLANATORY POWER OF FULL EQUATION   70%
```

Table 3.2
**Significant Predictors of Capital Police Expenditures,
Cities ≥ 50,000 Population, 1971**

```
CITY REVENUES        (+)

CITY CRIME RATE      (+)

POPULATION SIZE      (+)

PER CENT BLACK       (∼)*
```

```
EXPLANATORY POWER OF FULL EQUATION   22%
```

```
*(∼) CURVILINEAR RELATIONSHIP
```

Table 3.3
**Significant Predictors of Total Municipal Police Expenditures,
Cities < 50,000 Population, 1971**

```
CITY CRIME RATE      (+)

CITY REVENUES        (+)

PER CENT POOR        (-)

POPULATION DENSITY   (+)
```

```
EXPLANATORY POWER OF FULL EQUATION   60%
```

Table 3.4
Significant Predictors of Capital Police Expenditures,
Cities < 50,000 Population, 1971

```
        CITY CRIME RATE        (+)



EXPLANATORY POWER OF FULL EQUATION   9%
```

that during the early 1970s minority group size triggered white mobilization of capital policing resources increasingly until the size of the black population approached numerical majority (see Figure 3.1). This pattern may well have resulted from the availability of federal resources (LEAA funds) for capital policing items (cf. Jackson, 1986).

Small Cities

In the small city subgroup, percent black was not a significant predictor of

Figure 3.1
Relationship between 1971 Capital Police Expenditures and Percent Black in Cities ≥ 50,000 Population (N=281)

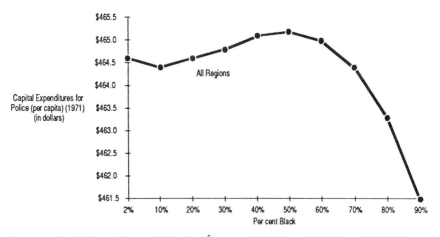

Note: Capital Expenditures, All Regions $\hat{Y}^* = -.02929X + .00191X^2 - .0000219X^3$.

    *   The values plotted include the sum of the constant term and the means of the independent variables in the estimating equation.

Source: This is a modified version of a figure originally published in Pamela Irving Jackson. (1986). "Black Visibility, City Size, and Social Control." *The Sociological Quarterly* 27 (2): 185-203. Reprinted with permission.

total or capital policing expenditures in 1970, and its impact just reached significance in the salaries/operations model. The variance explained in the small city models (60%, 63%, and 9% respectively for total, salaries/operations, and capital expenditures) is noticeably and significantly less than that explained by the models for the large city group (where the corresponding figures are 70%, 70%, and 22%). Furthermore, the polynomial terms for percent black do not add a statistically significant increment to the explained variance even for the capital expenditures equation, providing little support for the influence of minority group threat on the allocation of social control resources in cities under 50,000 in population size.

In 1971, then, the impact of percent black on policing expenditures differed in both form and strength in the large and small city groupings. The threat hypothesis appears to be supported by the data at the beginning of the decade in cities of 50,000 or more. Racial composition had a greater impact on public fiscal commitment to policing in large cities, where its impact on capital policing expenditures increased with the size of the minority population until the group reached numerical dominance. (Data for the end of the decade will be considered in Chapters 5 through 7.)

MINORITY COMPOSITION, POLICE EXPENDITURES, AND POLICE/COMMUNITY RELATIONS IN THE EARLY 1970s

Figure 3.2 provides minority composition and police expenditure comparisons for the 14 study cities, where local newspapers' portrayal of police and police/community relations are investigated. (Profiles of these cities' characteristics in 1970 and 1980 are contained in Chapters 5 through 7.) Seven of those cities—Baltimore, Newark, Detroit, Chicago, Philadelphia, Minneapolis, and Wichita (all outside the deep South and West)—are considered, beginning evaluation of the interrelations among city demographic characteristics, police expenditures, and police/community relations in the early 1970s.

The tone of newspaper reporting on policing in each city is discussed, and incidents that receive significant coverage are detailed as indicators of the view of the police that is presented to the public. Police brutality toward citizens, racial and ethnic biases in police hiring and promotions, mobilization of police resources, and minority/majority control over the police emerged as comparison points for the case studies. It may be that a city's structural characteristics, or the level or pattern of its policing expenditures are in some ways related to the public view reflected in the newspapers.

Capital expenditures in some of these seven cities, such as Baltimore and Philadelphia, were greater than their structural characteristics led us to expect.[2] In other cities, such as Detroit, Newark, Minneapolis, and Wichita, capital policing was underfunded in light of the city's structure and crime rate.

Figure 3.2
Comparisons of Minority Composition and Police Expenditures for Cities in Community Perceptions of Police Subpopulation

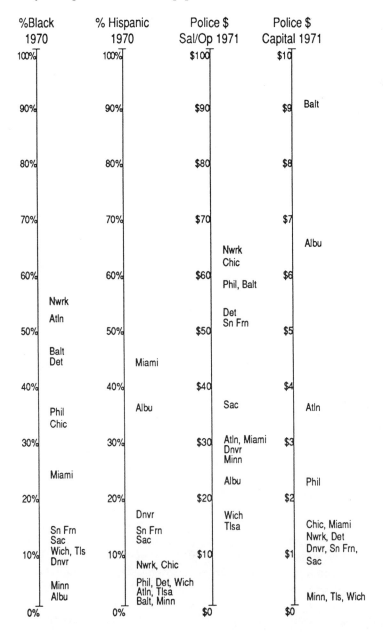

Detroit

The Context

At 84 crimes per thousand, Detroit's 1970 crime rate was over two and one-half times the large city average of 34 per thousand. Since Detroit's population of 1,511,000 in 1970 was about 44 percent black and 2 percent Hispanic, minority group interests were likely to become dominant at least numerically.

Revenues in Detroit, at $272 per capita, were only slightly (less than a standard deviation) higher than the $195 per capita average for cities of 50,000 or more. Eleven percent of the city's population was poor, about the same as the large city average of 10 percent. Given Detroit's high crime rate and population size in 1970, its above average level of reported expenditures for policing, at about $54 per capita overall for salaries, operations, and capital expenditures is not surprising.

Police Force: Racial Bias in Hiring and Promotion

Newspaper reports in Detroit in 1972 cited allegations of racism in the police department. For example, the president of the Guardians of Michigan (an organization of black law enforcement officers) charged both the Detroit Police Department and the Detroit Police Officers Association with institutional racism. Alleging that there were only 21 blacks on the list of 521 who qualified for promotion to sergeant, Moss stated that "Black Detroit policemen are denied promotions while men they have trained, many of whom are out and out racists are promoted" (*Michigan Chronicle*, 7/8/72). Moss indicated that the Guardians were about to seek an injunction against the Department to force (1) elimination of racial quotas in issuance of service ratings; (2) fair and equal treatment in disciplinary actions; (3) fair field supervision and assignments; (4) elimination of unfair hiring practices; (5) a more realistic standard regarding black officers' haircuts; and (6) the upgrading and assignment of more black precinct commanders.

Blacks clearly made some progress during the year, at least on the hiring front. November reporting (*Detroit Free Press*, 11/6/72; *Michigan Chronicle*, 11/25/72) described the Urban League's praise of the police department's hiring efforts, indicating that the percentage of black officers had risen from 3.8 percent in 1963 to 18.9 percent in 1972, and hailing increases in the assignment of black officers to top administrative positions. However, the Urban League pressed for more work in this direction, noting that while the same number of blacks and whites applied for police positions in 1971, five whites were accepted for every two blacks.

Police Brutality toward Citizens

Other articles relating to racial tensions in the police department focused not only on internal police force problems, but also on several instances of tension, hostility, and violence in white/black police officer interactions. An August 29 report, for example, described Police Commissioner Nichols' order that several white policemen be disciplined in connection with a July 22 incident in which they allegedly beat two black police officers who had attempted to stop police brutality toward a black citizen. In response to the charge that he was slow in responding in this case, Nichols was quoted as having said: "There is a difference in determining whether we are dealing with a real problem or a problem created by someone furthering their own personal aspirations . . . [some black officers have difficulty] becoming attuned to white supervision" (*Detroit Free Press*, 8/29/72).

In October a *Detroit Free Press* article, also describing an interview with Nichols over racial tensions in the police force, indicated that the main complaint of black police officers is that they do not like the way white officers treat black citizens and the way the department deals with black officers. Just a few months earlier, Chief Nichols had denied the existence of racism in the police department, but acknowledged that there were some bias and prejudice reflecting community attitudes (*Detroit Free Press*, 10/29/72).

Numerical equality in Detroit may have begun the struggle over police policy and poor treatment of black citizens. Black police officers had begun to protest rough police treatment of black citizens, and the way black officers were evaluated, assigned, and treated by white officers. The fact that black officers were organized, through the Guardian, is indicative of the stage that black involvement and efforts at minority control of the police had reached. Manifestations of the struggle over policy control included complaints about the evaluation, appearance code, assignment and disciplining of black officers (*Michigan Chronicle*, 7/8/72).

Police Expenditures and Black/White Control over the Police

Detroit's level of spending on policing was just about what our model predicted, $54 per capita. However, even after taking city revenues into account in the predicting equation, the city's level of capital police expenditures was about $1 per capita lower than predicted (a big discrepancy, since average per capita expenditures for capital items was about $2). At 44 percent of the population, Detroit blacks were numerically close to the majority. Hispanics constituted another 2 percent of the population. It may be that a well-equipped and well-armed police department was not a high priority of this minority population. Later chapters will demonstrate that official representatives from Detroit and other majority or close-to-majority black cities were soon to articulate this view. Detroit's lower than expected level of capital police spending may well have reflected the priorities of its almost majority minority population who had no need to mobilize police resources for dominance protection efforts.

Detroit blacks and whites had begun to struggle for control over police policy and administration. Despite a major riot in Detroit in the 1960s, city policing resources early in the 1970s were not being mobilized to stabilize traditional white dominance and order; rather, blacks, bolstered by near numerical control of the city, were beginning efforts at organizational control of the police.

Philadelphia

The Context

Philadelphia's 1970 population of 1,950,000 made the city one of the four largest in the group of cases under investigation. Yet the city's reported crime rate, at 23 per thousand, was below both the large and small city averages for 1970. The city was 34 percent black and 1.4 percent Hispanic. Policing expenditures were $60 per capita in 1972, $20 more per capita than predicted by our model, and on the high side even for a large city. Capital policing expenditures taken alone were, similarly, higher than expected ($2.20 per capita instead of $1.60).

Police Force: Racial Bias in Hiring and Promotions

Newspaper reports in Philadelphia in 1972 reflected charges of police brutality and underrepresentation of blacks on the police force. Federal Judge John P. Fullam, in view of the decline in the hiring of black police since 1966 (*Philadelphia Inquirer*, 5/26/72) issued an order requiring the police department to hire one black police officer for every two white recruits (*Philadelphia Inquirer*, 5/29/72). Figures indicated that the percentage of black police officers hired in a given year decreased from 27.5 percent in 1966 to 7.7 percent in 1970. In Fullam's words, "Continued use of hiring and promotion practices which discriminate against blacks causes irreparable injury to those discriminated against as well as to the public at large" (*Philadelphia Inquirer*, 7/8/72). The order was met with legal appeals and other forms of resistance by city and police officials (*Philadelphia Tribune*, 5/30/72; *Philadelphia Inquirer*, 5/31/72, 11/10/72).

Fraternal Order of Police President Gallagher and City Solicitor Martin Weinburg called Judge Fullam's decision "discrimination in reverse" (*Philadelphia Inquirer*, 5/29/72). They noted their opinion that the department had always tried to recruit blacks but found them uninterested because of the stigma of policing, and that black communities are usually hostile toward police officers whether they are black or white. The *Philadelphia Inquirer* (5/29/72) editorialized that black citizens are tired of "unjustified arrests and brutal harassment by policemen both white and black." The article continued: "In black communities the color of discrimination is blue—not black or white—and that is why it is so hard to find qualified black men who want to join the force."

Police Brutality toward Citizens

In April 1972, Mayor Rizzo "blasted" a report implying that Philadelphia police had used physical force without sufficient cause. He termed the report "biased, prejudiced, distorted, and unfair" and stated that it was directed at hurting his campaign for mayor (*Philadelphia Inquirer,* 4/4/72).

Specific allegations of police brutality appeared in the paper. The *Philadelphia Tribune* (8/15/72) reported that black public officials were demanding an investigation into police violence in black communities. These officials also opposed federal funds for additional police until what they alleged to be unequal treatment and violence ceased.

Mobilization of Police Resources

Mayor Rizzo, in an effort to put a "cop on every corner" and buy new equipment for the police department, applied for a large federal law enforcement grant to add officers and new equipment to the force (*Philadelphia Inquirer,* 6/25/72). Some questions were asked about it at the local level because the plans included putting large numbers of officers in low-crime rate areas. A special staff report recommended that nine patrolmen be assigned to each district for every 100 crimes reported each year. Police Commissioner Joseph F. O'Neill announced plans to bring all police districts up to normal patrol levels and then separate districts into "special tactical" units to concentrate on robbery and burglary. This action was expected to put more officers in low-crime areas. However, a study completed for the Philadelphia Regional Planning Council of the Governor's Justice Committee indicated that more police per capita would decrease the incidence of crime, and suggested that more police should be placed in high-crime areas (*Philadelphia Inquirer,* 9/13/72). A large LEAA grant ($4 million for the year) reportedly was obtained by Philadelphia (*Philadelphia Inquirer,* 10/5/72). Rizzo wanted to hire 63 police officers with it immediately, and hire 1,500 before his first term was up. [Earlier reporting had indicated that the court order requiring the Philadelphia Police Department to hire one black officer for every two white recruits was a major impediment to a positive federal decision on the city's grant application (*Philadelphia Tribune,* 7/18/72).]

Police Expenditures and Black/White Control of the Police

As the size of Philadelphia's minority population in the early 1970s led us to expect, after one riot, policing resources in the city were being mobilized with an orientation toward crime control and maintenance of order. Although Philadelphia's reported crime rate was not high, the city's level of policing expenditures was much higher than expected; there was considerable discussion of problems of racially motivated police brutality and imposition of a federal court order to increase the number of blacks on the force.

The city's mayor pursued a tough law-and-order, anti-crime policy in word and deed. Newspaper reporting about city police did not focus on the development of community relations efforts or on the need for police-provided services to citizens. Rather, the focus was on the need for crime control and efforts to obtain funds for more officers and equipment. A struggle for dominance and control over city police services was being waged; even federal efforts to integrate the city's police force were being resisted. At this point whites still had the upper hand.

Baltimore

The Context

Despite their numbers, Baltimore blacks had not attained the kind of administrative and policy control of policing that was characteristic of Detroit. In Baltimore, with 46 percent black and 1 percent Hispanic, $58 per capita were reported to have been spent on police salaries and operations, while $9 per capita were spent on capital policing items. On the basis of the city's demographic characteristics and crime rate, capital expenditures were greater than expected by about $6 per capita. The overall crime rate, at 69 crimes per thousand, was quite high.

Baltimore was a large city with a 1970 population of about 906,000. At $618 per capita, its revenues were over three times the average for large cities, and its rate of poverty, about 14 percent, was on the high side as well.

Mobilization of Police Resources

In 1972 Donald Pomerleau was reappointed to another six-year term as police commissioner. He had been police commissioner since 1966. Although the governor cited him for his leadership in transforming the Baltimore Police Department into one of the finest in the country, the minority community was not enthusiastic. One hundred black leaders demanded that the governor fire Pomerleau for being unwilling to meet and discuss problems of the city's ghettos (*Sun*, 5/20/72).

Commissioner Pomerleau indicated that the help of the community and about 200 more police officers were needed to bring down the city's crime rate. In response to questions about the black community's criticism of him, Pomerleau admitted to having made mistakes, but noted that he had "shown willingness to correct these mistakes" (*Sun*, 5/29/72).

News reporting also focused on two helicopters purchased by the Baltimore Police Department (*Sun*, 3/12/72); some citizens referred to them as "spies in the skies" that make people feel like "fish in a bowl." Discussed in an article entitled "City Police Praise Their Air Force," these helicopters were described as a crime deterrent and an aid in the apprehension of criminals.

Police Brutality toward Citizens

In January 1972, a *Sun* article entitled "Police Probes of Brutality Charges Leave Complainants Unsatisfied" (1/27/72a) described a survey of 20 victims of alleged police brutality within the preceding 2 years indicating that complainants felt they had not received justice through the police department's Internal Investigation Division. A victim of one incident claimed that "the Internal Investigation Division is designed to placate people until things blow over."

Another article in the same paper, "One Accused Policeman in Four is Found Guilty" (*Sun*, 1/27/72b), noted the results of a police department investigation of 437 policemen the previous year on charges ranging from discourtesy to excessive force. Disciplinary action ranged from a warning to a dismissal. Of the 64 policemen accused of using excessive force, 5 were found guilty. The most common charge in 1971, the article stated, was misconduct, and one-third of the 145 men so charged were found guilty. Since 1965 the percentage of sustained allegations had ranged from 25 percent to 28 percent, the latter figure being for 1971. Many specific incidents were reported. For example, in November, two patrolmen charged with racist actions resigned from the force. Other investigations of brutality appeared in news reporting during 1972 (*Sun* 1/6/72, 4/15/72, 11/28/72, 12/4/72).

Black/White Control over the Police

The fact that so much police-related reporting focused on brutality charges and so little on black control of the police may have resulted from Baltimore's location. As the analysis in Chapter 4 will demonstrate, the southern threat curve was more pronounced than the national curve of the percent black/capital police expenditures relationship. Blacks in Baltimore may have made less progress than Detroit blacks in assuming control over police department personnel and procedures despite the similarity in the relative size of each city's black population largely because of the informal social controls exerted by the history and biases of the South.

Chicago

The Context

With a population of 3,367,000 in 1970, Chicago was the largest city in the set of case studies. At that time blacks were 33 percent of the population and Hispanics 7 percent. Policing expenditures for salaries and operations, at about $61 per capita, were about at the predicted level, while capital expenditures' at $1.40 per capita, were less than the $2.10 predicted by our equation. City revenues ($183 per capita) were slightly below the large city average, while the rate of poverty was just about average at 10.6 percent. Chicago had had four riots between 1966 and 1970.

Police Brutality toward Citizens

Newspaper reporting in Chicago in 1972 was fraught with instances of reported police abuse, investigations of raids on the Black Panthers, and complaints regarding Police Superintendent Conlisk. Nevertheless, Mayor Daley supported Conlisk, whose policy of "aggressive preventive patrol" had come under considerable public criticism by black leaders who alleged that the policy led to the harassment of blacks and contributed to police brutality and black oppression. (See, for example, *Chicago Tribune*, 5/13/72; *Chicago Daily News*, 6/26/72; *Chicago Sun-Times*, 6/27/72). Superintendent Conlisk repeatedly defended the policy as effective in reducing major crimes in the city.

Allegations of racially related police brutality and discrimination in Chicago included the death of a black dentist (reportedly erroneously detained for over five hours on drunk driving charges) as a result of symptoms produced by a stroke that took his life possibly for lack of prompt medical treatment due to police detainment (*Chicago Tribune*, 4/29/72); the beating of a pregnant black woman leading to the loss of her baby (*Daily Defender*, 4/1/72); and the beating, by several officers, of a black man handcuffed to a fence (*Daily Defender*, 1/24/72).

Public Hearings and Lawsuits

A May 1972 report in the *Chicago Sun-Times* (5/18/72) indicated that the city council ordered hearings on police brutality in the face of public charges of widespread harassment of blacks and other minorities by some policemen. The *Chicago Tribune* (5/18/72) ran an article at the same time entitled, "Conlisk Orders Policemen to Stop Harassing Latins." The article reported that Conlisk's action was in response to complaints voiced by Latin Americans that police were checking immigration papers. To demonstrate brutality on the part of Chicago police officers, civic, community, civil rights, racial equality and other groups prepared 25 case histories for review by a federal grand jury (*Chicago Sun-Times*, 3/31/72). The Chicago Human Relations Commission continued study of 23 of the 91 cases of brutality submitted to it (*Chicago Daily News*, 7/24/72).

Black Panther Indictments

Throughout the year Chicago's history of tense police/community relations surfaced in reporting in the *Chicago Daily News* (6/12/72, 7/11/72), the *Chicago Sun-Times* (5/16/72, 5/31/72), the *Chicago Tribune* (5/16/72, 7/6/72, 7/11/72), and the *Daily Defender* (7/11/72a) relating to conspiracy indictments for covering up evidence regarding the December 4, 1969 raid in which two Panther leaders were killed. Fourteen law enforcement officials were indicted for allegedly falsifying and destroying information presented to a federal grand jury relating to the number of shots fired and alleged unlawful acts by the police in that incident.

In December 1972, three civil rights groups and seven persons filed suit against Police Superintendent Conlisk, charging the department with encouraging police brutality. The suit sought a court order forcing Conlisk to adopt an effective police discipline system, including citizen investigation in an open atmosphere of complaints lodged by citizens against the police (see *Chicago Sun-Times,* 12/23/72).

Police Force: Racial Discrimination in Hiring and Promotions

The president of the city's Afro-American Patrolmen's League asked in September for a freeze of federal funds to Chicago police until alleged civil rights violations were corrected. The letter was directed to LEAA, and requested a cut of $10 million to $20 million in funding to the city (*Chicago Sun-Times,* 9/1/72). In response LEAA determined that the Chicago police force did not intentionally discriminate against its black and Spanish speaking members, but needed to change hiring, training, and promotion practices (*Chicago Sun-Times,* 9/6/72). The Patrolmen's League president asked for a court order to force Chicago police to comply with LEAA's suggestions. There was much discussion of the need for civilian review boards, and for promotions of black officers into higher level ranks (see for example, *Chicago Courier,* 9/22/72; *Chicago Sun-Times,* 12/4/72, 12/7/72, 12/8/72; *Chicago Tribune,* 4/25/72, 5/5/72, 5/6/72, 5/31/72; *Daily Defender,* 4/25/72, 7/11/72b, 12/7/72).

Black/White Control over the Police

In the early 1970s, continued white domination of the Chicago police seemed assured. Despite federal hearings and highly publicized complaints regarding present and past racial discrimination and brutality toward black citizens, as well as complaints about the roadblocks preventing black and Hispanic police officers from professional advancement, whites remained in control of the police. Even in the face of public pressure from minorities, Mayor Daley and Police Commissioner Conlisk refused to question the Chicago Police Department's policy of "aggressive preventive patrol," and no new plans for the advancement of minority officers or toward improvement in police/minority relations were put forward. As in Philadelphia, another city where about one-third of the population was black, minority groups in Chicago had not succeeded in establishing effective measures of control over policies of police recruitment or police/community relations.

Newark

The Context

A city of 382,000 in 1970, Newark was a majority black city. In fact, with 54 percent of its residents black and 7 percent Hispanic, close to two-thirds of the city's population was minority. While the level of poverty at 18 percent reflected the minority status of its residents, the city's level of overall revenues was not extremely low ($425 per capita). Its crime rate, however, was quite high at 83 crimes per thousand; police expenditures were also on the high side, about $5.5 greater than predicted by the equations based on the city's socioeconomic characteristics. Capital police expenditures taken alone, however, at $1.20 per capita were about $1 per capita less than expected.

Police Brutality toward Citizens

Newspaper reports relating to police/community relations or to police funding in Newark were sparse in 1972. The *Newark Evening News* (4/28/72) reported in April that Mayor Gibson had ordered Newark's police director to request an F.B.I. investigation into the alleged beatings of five Puerto Rican youths by police to see if police had used unnecessary force in the situation and violated the youths' civil rights. Other reporting focused on charges that a black postal employee had been beaten by police after witnessing a patrolman hitting a black, handcuffed man (*Newark Evening News*, 5/30/72, 6/2/72).

Police brutality had a long history in Newark. On the basis of their investigation of crime and politics in Newark, Heinz et al. (1983: 65) conclude that despite continuous public pressure to control police brutality, three problems persisted: (1) Officers shot those who fled and beat those they arrested; (2) investigation of those officers involved was superficial; and (3) law-abiding people feared the police.

Black/White Control over the Police

Newark's first black mayor was elected in 1970. Blacks' sense of identification with Mayor Gibson and their sense of ownership over the city's government may account for the relatively low level of police related public clamor in 1972. In fact, despite a $20 million LEAA grant to Newark (one of the eight cities targeted by the agency's High Impact Anti-Crime Program) to be spent in two years, the 1970s witnessed a decline in public support for the police by the city's political leaders. The LEAA funds available to the city beginning in 1972 and continuing until the middle of the decade led to the development of new community relations projects, and some new hiring of police officers. As Chapter 5 describes, with the last of the LEAA funds toward the close of the decade, the city's lack of commitment toward policing became clear in its failure to assume continuation costs for the programs and personnel.

Minneapolis

The Context

As its position in Figure 3.2 indicates, Minneapolis was at the low end of the minority visibility range, spent relatively little for capital police items, and had a relatively low level of policing expenditures in general. Its crime rate of 54 per thousand was over one standard deviation above the 1970 mean for large cities, but not excessively high. With a black population of about 4 percent and Hispanic population groups constituting less than 1 percent of the population, minority threat may not have reached an influential level despite Minneapolis' large size in 1970 (434,000). In comparison to the values predicted by the national expenditures equations, the city spent about $6 per capita less than expected on policing overall in 1971, and about $1 per capita less on capital items.

In terms of both spending and public attention, policing was not in the forefront of Minneapolis' concerns early in the decade. Newspaper reporting in 1972 on police expenditures and police/community relations in Minneapolis was limited to a brief December discussion of the police manpower-use policy of shifting injured officers to non-police functions (*Minneapolis Tribune*, 12/27/72), and discussions in May and August of an alleged police attack on anti-war protestors and bystanders during May demonstrations at the University of Minnesota (*Minneapolis Tribune*, 5/24/72, 8/28/72). Racial biases in the hiring and promotion of minority police officers, police brutality toward citizens, and black versus white control over the police were not the focus of discussion in Minneapolis' newspapers at the time.

Wichita

The Context

At 10 percent black and 2.5 percent Hispanic in 1970, the size of Wichita's minority population was not large enough to encourage development of a high level of minority group threat. However, the city had had two riots at the end of the previous decade—sufficient turmoil to polarize the racial groups in any community. A city of 277,000, Wichita had more interracial income inequality (0.62) lower than average for large cities (0.67). Its rate of poverty (8.2%) was a bit lower than the large city average, and overall revenues ($159 per capita) were also slightly under the expected average level. The crime rate, 40 per thousand population, was also greater than the national large city average (34 per thousand). The city's spending for police salaries and operations ($16 per capita) and capital police expenditures ($.30 per capita) was considerably below expected levels.

Newspaper reports of racial or ethnic conflicts between police and the community were not evident. Police-related reporting in Wichita in 1972 centered on limited reports concerning the development of a police/community relations advisory committee (*Wichita Eagle*, 2/11/72, 2/18/72, 2/23/72) and several community-related programs such as Officer Friendly, motorcycle training for teens, and interracial softball competitions. It could be that the city's riots in the 1960s contributed to the early 1970s' police force emphasis on building rapport with the community. Public scrutiny of police/minority relations was actually greater in Wichita by the end of the decade than it was at the beginning (see Chapter 6).

IMPLICATIONS

Early in the 1970s the impact of minority size on public commitment to social control had two major manifestations nationally. First, municipal fiscal resources were influenced by the relative size of the city's black population, even after the crime rate and social context of the community are taken into consideration. In fact, for capital police expenditures, fiscal support for policing increased until blacks constituted a majority of the city's population, then dropped off (even after the inclusion of controls for city revenues and poverty) as if to indicate blacks' loss of concern and loss of faith in the merits of equipping police forces with capital resources.

Second, the tone and focus of events and activities concerning police/ community relations were influenced by the relative size of the black community. In Minneapolis and Wichita, both less than 10 percent black, the black community may not have been a major factor in police hiring and procedural policies, despite the riots in both cities in the 1960s. The greatest hostility and tension were apparent in cities like Philadelphia and Chicago (in which blacks constituted about one-third of the population) where battles of dominance over police force hiring and procedures and over city politics itself were still being waged.

Where control was more clearly in the hands of one side or the other—as in Detroit and Newark, with their majority or close-to-majority black populations, or in Minneapolis and Wichita, where less than 10 percent of the population was black—the acrimony in police/community relations was either not present or had begun to subside. In Detroit, for example, public police-related discussion focused on black control over personnel and policy of the city police force. In Newark, the election of a black mayor in 1970 seemed to eclipse earlier public clamor about police brutality as the city set to work to make it a problem of the past. Baltimore deviates from these findings with continued mobilization of police resources and white domination of the police force despite the close-to-majority size of the black population. It provides a prelude to Chapter 4, which focuses on the influence of regional context in minority/majority struggles for control over police resources and policy. Given its proximity to the South, Baltimore may be a city in which the cultural context of the region filtered not only whites' perceptions of the minority, but also blacks' perceptions of what is possible and their tolerance of white political control as well. We now turn our attention to the influence of region on the relationship between minority group presence and social control.

NOTES

1. For exceptions, see Jackson, 1985, 1986. Greenberg, Kessler, and Loftin (1983), in a study of police employment and crime, developed a model including percent black and tested the model separately in cities of 50,000 or more in 1960 and in a sample of 252

northern and northeastern suburbs for which Huff and Stahura (1980) had gathered data on police employment and suburban crime. Huff and Stahura (1980: 463) had operationally defined "suburb" as "an incorporated place with a population of 10,000 or more, located within the bounds of a standard metropolitan statistical area, but outside of its central city." The regional limitation of their sample was imposed by a lack of data for a sufficient number of southern and western suburbs. This regional limitation and the limitations imposed by the "suburban" definition make it impossible to draw inferences about the determinants of collective social control efforts in cities of 25,000 to 50,000 on the basis of the Greenberg et al. study.

2. The ordinary least-squares regression equations described in this chapter (and presented in detail in the tables of the Appendix) provide estimates for each city of the level of police expenditures expected on the basis of the city's crime rate and sociodemographic characteristics. As Tables 3.1 and 3.2 indicate, and as is customary in social science research, the regression equations did not explain all of the variance in either expenditures for police salaries and operations or capital expenditures. The difference between the level of expenditures predicted by the equation and actual police expenditures for each city results from idiosyncratic variations between cities and/or the omission of expenditure determinants in the model. The case study analyses are intended to stimulate thought about these idiosyncrasies or possible omissions.

Predicted values for each city reflect the level of expenditures expected on the basis of the city's sociodemographic characteristics and crime rate if the impact of these characteristics in the city conforms to the expectations of the model. For an individual city the difference between actual and predicted police expenditures represents the magnitude of the difference between the actual determinants of police expenditures in the city and the pattern established in the model developed on the basis of the data for the aggregate of cities. These differences are sometimes considerable. For example, as discussed in the text, in the case of capital expenditures, where the need for automobiles and improvements to physical facilities may influence spending, the predictive power of the model was much weaker than that for police salaries and operations.

4

Across the Nation: Variations in Hostility and Social Control

Although recent study of variations in the level of collective commitment to social control suggests that efforts to control the activity of a minority group escalate as its threat to asymmetrical social and economic exchange relationships increases (cf. Jacobs, 1979), this literature does not demonstrate that the police are used as a repressive force. However, it is likely that the conditions conducive to such use exist throughout the United States.

In each region of the country there is at least one minority group viewed by politically dominant groups as threatening because of historical prejudice and demonstrative political activity. In the absence of assertive prevention efforts, these intergroup biases will, like other socially determined and transmitted values, be reflected in the attitudes of those members of the social system who are directly responsible for crime control in the community—that is, the police. Recent research suggests that even fiscally stressed cities find the funds necessary to expand policing resources when politically motivated to do so (cf. Heinz et al., 1983). Minority group size and fear of crime, which is exacerbated by the presence of a culturally or racially dissimilar minority group, provide such motivation.

This chapter investigates the extent to which regional context influences the link between minority group size and public fiscal support for social control. Two sets of evidence will be reviewed: (1) the impact of percent Hispanic on municipal police expenditures in cities of the South and West in contrast to northeastern and north central cities and (2) the impact of percent black on policing resources in southern cities.

THE IMPORTANCE OF REGION

Regional context has important implications for the degree of minority/majority competition for sociopolitical dominance and for the perception of minority group threat. Tables 2.4-2.7 indicate persistent regional variations in the size of minority populations, with a greater percentage of blacks in southern cities and a larger percentage of Hispanic ethnic group members in cities of the South and West. Minority/majority conflict has been most tense in the regions where minority numbers are greatest, as explained by Blalock's (1967) work linking majority group resource mobilization efforts to the relative size of the minority group. The level of income inequality between blacks and whites is greatest in the southern and southern/western groups of cities, and poverty has been somewhat more extensive in the South.

Exacerbating the problems associated with regional variations in the sociohistorical traditions of minority/majority conflict are the persistent regional variations in crime rates. Crime rates are highest in the South and in cities of the West, and they have been for decades (cf. Brantingham and Brantingham, 1984; Pyle, 1976; Harries, 1971, 1974; Kowalski et al., 1980). This pattern of variation, with violent crime particularly high in the South, has been seen as a cultural phenomenon by some, and a result of sociodemographic patterns by others (cf. Gastil, 1971; Hackney, 1969; Loftin and Hill, 1974). Regional variations in crime contribute to variations in collective commitment to social control, as do variations in the fear of crime, a social phenomenon related not only to the actual rate of crime, but to the degree of interracial victimization and minority group visibility as well.

Fear of Crime and Minority Group Size

The literature on fear of crime identifies minority group size and visibility, segregation, and perception of the likelihood of interracial victimization along with overall crime rates as influential determinants of the level of public commitment to social control.

Research by Liska, Lawrence, and Benson (1981) and by Liska, Lawrence, and Sanchirico (1982) indicates that whites' fear of crime is positively related to the presence and visibility of a culturally dissimilar minority group. This is partly a result of the triggering of racial stereotypes of nonwhites as a criminal element, a problem exacerbated by increases in the level of interracial crime. It is reasonable to expect, then, that regional variations in the intensity of racial stereotypes are reflected in varying levels of fear of crime.

Theoretical work by Blalock (1967) and empirical work by Jackson and Carroll (1981) and Jackson (1985, 1986) also suggest a link between fear of crime and fear of minority group mobilization efforts. When minority groups are involved in demonstrative political activity, municipal support for social control varies positively with the size of the minority population, until the group approaches numerical majority. At that point, the level of social control commitment declines markedly, possibly because questions of political dominance have been resolved.

Hispanics in the South and West

The Census Bureau's Hispanic designation incorporates several ethnic groups, including Puerto Ricans, Mexican-Americans, Colombians, Dominicans, Cubans, and Continental Spaniards. In 1970, Mexican-Americans were the predominant Hispanic group in the Southwest, with sizable proportions in the Midwest and Northwest as well; Puerto Ricans constituted the largest Hispanic ethnic group in the Northeast, although some Colombians, Dominicans, Cubans, and Continental Spaniards were present in this region; in the Southeast, especially Florida, Cubans were the core of the Hispanic population.

Political activism by New York area Puerto Ricans surfaced in the 1960s whereas Mexican-American protest activity in the West and Southwest was evident early in the twentieth century when strikes and other economic protests occurred in California, Idaho, Washington, Colorado, and Texas. During the 1950s and 1960s Mexican-Americans were mobilized and organized through the Alinsky inspired Community Services Organization and the National Farm Workers' Association led by Cesar Chavez. The activities of Mexican-American farm laborers brought national attention to the plight of Mexican-Americans and their subordinate economic and political position. That, in combination with the size (10 percent versus 2.8 percent in northeastern and north central cities) and ethnic and political unity of the predominant Hispanic ethnic groups in cities of the South and West, enhanced this group's visibility and cultural distinctiveness in 1970, thereby contributing to its threat in cities of the South and West.

Growth of the relative size of Hispanic population groups continued during the 1970s, increasing by 2 percent in cities of the South and West and by about 1 percent in northeastern and north central cities. Overall, the Hispanic population located in U.S. cities of 25,000 or more grew by about 1 percent during the decade. This continued growth of Hispanic populations, combined with reductions in interracial violence during the decade, may have focused greater national attention on Hispanics, and on the degree of threat to prevailing cultural standards posed by their increasing presence in the population.

Blacks in the South

The historically subordinate position of blacks in the South has persisted to the present day. As Tables 2.6 and 2.7 indicate, the 1980 U.S. Census estimated that blacks constituted, on average, 25 percent of the population of southern cities, regardless of size. Their relative economic position, as reflected in the ratio of black to white median income, was worse in these cities than in any other region, despite recent migration of economic opportunities to the Sunbelt (cf.

Goodman, 1979). The proportion of blacks in southern urban populations grew slightly between 1970 and 1980 by 2% in large southern cities, and by 5% overall in small southern cities). There was also some reduction in the level of inequality between southern blacks and whites during the period, with blacks earning, on average, just under two-thirds of whites' average income in large southern cities, as opposed to just over one-half in 1970, and 58 percent in small southern cities, up 2 percent from 1970. However, given the considerable inequality between blacks and whites in the South and the history of their relations in the region, it is likely that tension between them did not dissipate by the end of the decade, despite changes in the federal climate relating to law and order issues.

This chapter investigates the 1971 regional variations in the influence of minority size on public fiscal commitment to policing. It is expected that percent black had its greatest impact on policing resources in the South, especially in large cities. The lower level of anonymity and greater social cohesion characteristic of smaller cities may have reduced the degree of threat triggered by blacks and increased the effect of informal social controls, thereby weakening the relationship between the size of the black population and the level of public fiscal commitment to policing. End-of-the-decade comparisons are discussed in Chapter 7.

RESULTS

Hispanic Population Groups

Tables 4.1-4.4 illustrate the impact of the relative size of the Hispanic population on the level of policing resources at the end of the 1970s, after other sociodemographic predictors have been controlled (see Tables A.8, A.9, and A.10 for more detailed information). As expected, percent Hispanic had a

Table 4.1
Significant Predictors of Total Municipal Police Expenditures, Southern and Western Cities, 1971

CITY REVENUES	(+)
CITY CRIME RATE	(+)
PER CENT POOR	(−)
PER CENT BLACK	(+)
POPULATION DENSITY	(+)
PER CENT HISPANIC	(+)

EXPLANATORY POWER OF FULL EQUATION   71%

Table 4.2
Significant Predictors of Capital Police Expenditures,
Southern and Western Cities, 1971

```
              CITY CRIME RATE      (+)

              CITY REVENUES        (+)

              PER CENT HISPANIC    (∿)*


    EXPLANATORY POWER OF FULL EQUATION   25%


        *(∿) CURVILINEAR RELATIONSHIP
```

Table 4.3
Significant Predictors of Total Municipal Police Expenditures,
Northern and North Central Cities, 1971

```
              CITY REVENUES           (+)

              PER CENT BLACK          (+)

              POPULATION DENSITY      (-)

              POPULATION SIZE         (+)

              CITY CRIME RATE         (+)

              INTER-RACIAL INEQUALITY (+)


    EXPLANATORY POWER OF FULL EQUATION   78%
```

Table 4.4
Significant Predictors of Capital Police Expenditures,
Northern and North Central Cities, 1971

```
              PER CENT BLACK       (+)

              POPULATION SIZE      (+)

              CITY REVENUES        (+)

              PER CENT HISPANIC    (-)


    EXPLANATORY POWER OF FULL EQUATION   27%
```

positive, significant impact on police expenditures in southern and western cities in 1971, while its influence in northern and north central cities was limited to a negative impact on capital policing expenditures. In both regional subpopulations, other elements determining the magnitude of urban policing expenditures were percent black, the city's fiscal capacity, the crime rate, community size, and density.

In the southern and western city subpopulation, where prejudice against Hispanics has historically been greatest, the impact of percent Hispanic on capital policing expenditures in 1971 was best expressed by a curvilinear function whose shape supported Blalock's (1967) proposition that public willingness to control a minority group's activity increases with the group's visibility and threat to existing patterns of dominance (cf. Jackson, 1985). (See Figure 4.1.) The fact that the impact of percent poor on policing expenditures was negative and statistically significant in the southern and western city subpopulation indicates that the services provided by the police to low income individuals were not the source of the link between percent Hispanic and police expenditures. The presence of a large poor population reduced spending on police salaries and operations, but had no significant impact on spending for capital items.

Black Populations

Comparison of the early-in-the-decade findings in Tables 4.5-4.8 (see also Tables A.5 and A.6) indicates that as in the national population of cities (see Tables A.3 and A.4), percent black was a statistically significant predictor of policing expenditures in large southern cities, but not in small southern cities. For capital expenditures, however, the 1970 southern results were noticeably different in two ways. First, the linear model has more explanatory power

Table 4.5
Significant Predictors of Total Municipal Police Expenditures, Southern Cities ≥ 50,000 Population, 1971

```
POPULATION DENSITY    (+)

CRIME RATE            (+)

PER CENT BLACK        (+)

PER CENT POOR         (-)

CITY REVENUES         (+)
```

```
EXPLANATORY POWER OF FULL EQUATION   70%
```

Figure 4.1
Relationship between 1971 Capital Police Expenditures and Percent Hispanic in All Cities (N=317) and in Southern and Western Cities (N=175)

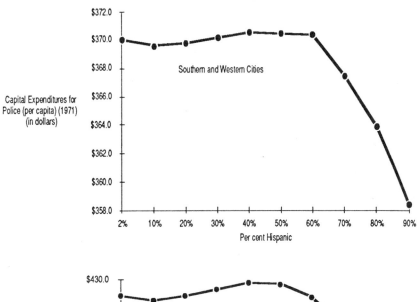

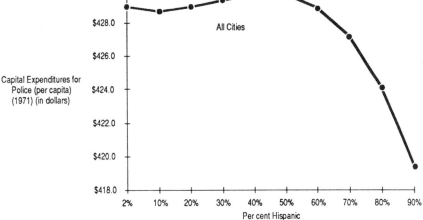

Note: All cities $\hat{Y}^* = -.06006X + .00398X^2 - .00005X^3$.
           Southern and Western Cities $\hat{Y}^* = -.08351X + .00481X^2 - .00006X^3$.

     * The values plotted include the sum of the constant term and the means of the independent variables in the estimating equation.

Source: This is a rescaled version of a figure originally published in Pamela Irving Jackson. (1985). "Ethnicity, Region, and Public Fiscal Commitment to Policing." *Justice Quarterly* 2(2):167-194. Reprinted with permission of the Academy of Criminal Justice Sciences.

Table 4.6
Significant Predictors of Capital Police Expenditures,
Southern Cities ≥ 50,000 Population, 1971

```
POPULATION DENSITY   (+)

CITY REVENUE         (+)

PER CENT BLACK       (∼)*
```

```
EXPLANATORY POWER OF FULL EQUATION   48%
```

```
*(∼) CURVILINEAR RELATIONSHIP
```

Table 4.7
Significant Predictors of Total Municipal Police Expenditures,
Southern Cities < 50,000 Population, 1971

```
CITY CRIME RATE       (+)

CITY REVENUES         (+)

PER CENT POOR         (-)

POPULATION DENSITY    (+)

INTER-RACIAL INEQUALITY (-)
```

```
EXPLANATORY POWER OF FULL EQUATION   53%
```

Table 4.8
Significant Predictors of Capital Police Expenditures,
Southern Cities < 50,000 Population, 1971

```
CITY CRIME RATE       (+)
```

```
EXPLANATORY POWER OF FULL EQUATION   26%
```

(explaining about 20% more variance) in the southern large-city group than in the national group of large cities; second, recognizing the curvilinear form of the percent black/capital expenditures relationship (including the polynomial terms for percent black in the equation) added 7 percent to the variance explained in the South (while it increased by only 1% the variance explained in large cities nationally).

In addition, the minority group threat/capital expenditures curve was more pronounced in southern than in the general large city subpopulation (see Tables A.2 and A.5, and Figures 3.1 and 4.2). The shape of the curves in both cases indicated positive nonlinear increases in capital policing expenditures from 10 percent to 40 percent black, further increases at a lower rate until blacks constituted a majority of the population, and then a precipitous drop-off where the minority had achieved numerical dominance. The pattern of this relationship suggests a mobilization of social control resources until the relative size of the black population approaches or exceeds that of whites (cf. Jackson, 1986). Thus, in 1971, while the South was much like the rest of the country in the determinants of municipal police spending, the impact of percent black on the level of spending was, as expected, greater in this region.

Figure 4.2
Relationship between 1971 Capital Police Expenditures and Percent Black in Southern Cities ≥ 50,000 Population

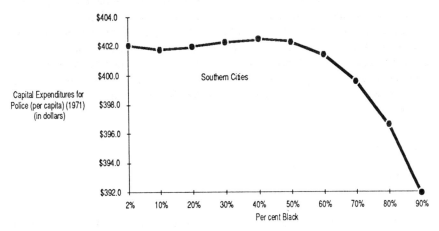

Note: Capital Expenditures, Southern Cities (N=85)
         $\hat{Y}* = -.06315X + .00367X^2 - .0000469X^3$.

   * The values plotted include the sum of the constant term and the means of the variables in the estimating equation.

Source: This is a modified version of a figure originally published in Pamela Irving Jackson. (1986). "Black Visibility, City Size, and Social Control." *The Sociological Quarterly* 27(2): 185-203. Reprinted with permission.

None of the information presented in the national and regional analyses demonstrates that the police are a repressive force toward blacks in southern cities or toward Hispanics in southern and western cities. Evidence to support or refute that contention could only be generated through a detailed analysis of law enforcement activities within individual cities. However, the evidence at hand does suggest greater collective commitment to policing in urban centers most likely to be characterized by a struggle for dominance—in regions where the minority group is, for historical reasons, likely to be viewed as threatening, and in cities in which the group is large enough to constitute a threat.

The role of the police deserves special consideration in regional settings that have, for sociohistorical reasons, potentially explosive patterns of intergroup relations. In the remainder of this chapter investigation focuses on some of the individual cities in these regions—their demographic settings and the perceptions of local police activity that emerge in their newspapers. In these case studies we will look for the influence of minority size and region on public expectations for the police.

THE FILTERING EFFECT OF REGION ON THE LINK BETWEEN MINORITY COMPOSITION AND POLICE/COMMUNITY RELATIONS

In this section, discussion of policing and social structure in several southern and western cities illustrates the findings of the national study and provides a reasonably representative picture of the importance of regional location, urban structural characteristics, and crime rates on the level of police resource mobilization and on the nature of police/community relations. Miami, Atlanta, and Tulsa are examined to detect the influence of the South's historical bias against blacks on the link between the relative size of this population and public commitment to policing. San Francisco, Sacramento, Denver, and Albuquerque are reviewed to assess the importance of the Hispanic threat in the West and Southwest.

THE SOUTH

Miami

The Context

A city of 335,000 in 1970, Miami was about 23 percent black and 45 percent Hispanic. Yet as evident in the following discussion, any review of police/community relations in Miami must focus primarily on conflicts between blacks and whites. Blacks earned, on average, 73 percent of whites' income, and the incidence of poverty (16%) in the city was much higher than the national urban average (10%). City revenues, at $147 per capita, were below the large city average of $195 per capita. The city's crime rate was twice the national average at 71 crimes per thousand. Police expenditures, at $32 per capita, were about $1.50 less than expected overall, while capital expenditures were a bit above the level predicted on the basis of the city's socioeconomic characteristics at $1.40 per capita.

Police Force: Discrimination in Hiring and Promotion

Police-related reporting in Miami in 1972 focused on: (1) a discrimination suit against the city by black officers alleging past discriminatory practices on the part of the Miami Police Department (*Miami Times*, 10/23/72); (2) the Miami Police Benevolent Association's loss of its bid to remain all white, and the U.S. Supreme Court's refusal to overturn lower court rulings on this matter (*Miami Times*, 10/11/72, 10/19/72); and (3) the dismissal of two white officers for subjecting two black prisoners to "sadistic torture tactics" (*Miami Herald*, 12/28/72).

On the matter of the Police Benevolent Association's loss of its court battles to remain all white, a *Miami Times* (10/19/72) editorial exulted, admonishing the PBA for its "long time racist stand," charging that it "has directly contributed to the division facing our community and has led to the record high crime rate with which we are faced . . . [and that] citizens cannot be expected to respect policemen whose racism is so blatant."

Police Brutality toward Citizens

Several months later, the *Miami Times* (12/22/72), heralding "Police-Community Relations to Improve," voiced its approval of the City of Miami's dismissal of two white officers for brutality. Calling itself "the chief critic of police community relations as they affect the Miami Police and . . . the black community," the editorial credited Police Chief Gamin with having undertaken within his command to rid the force of old-line and maladjusted officers to whom brutality was a way of life, a tool necessary for the handling of poor minorities." The *Times* expressed its hope that this action would serve to "ease existing animosity toward the force—especially among young blacks—and bridge what was an ever widening chasm between them and the police department."

Mobilization of Police Resources

There was also some reporting on the city's failure to win one of the LEAA high impact anti-crime awards, indicating that the city's mismanagement of some funds from a previous LEAA anti-crime grant and Greater Miami's complicated governmental structure may have been at fault. The latter consisted of 27 cities, "each going its own way in law enforcement. The jerry-built crime-fighting effort has duplicating communications systems, individual boundaries, procedures made costly because of overlap and inevitable jealousies . . ." (*Miami Herald*, 1/15/72).

*Expenditures for Policing and Minority/Majority
Control over the Police*

Although about one-third of the Miami Police Department's 800 officer force
was black (*Miami Herald,* 11/9/72), the exclusion of blacks from the Police
Benevolent Association underscored their subordinate position within the
department and their limited impact on police policy and procedures. While
blacks were included on the force in 1972, their influence did not seem to match
the level of their numerical inclusion. The fact that blacks were effectively
controlled through their inclusion without policy impact may have contributed
to the relatively low level of policing expenditures in this minority dominated
community. It may be that the relatively low level of police expenditures in
Miami reflected the largely minority population's general demoralization
concerning the effectiveness and desirability of policing. However, it is also
possible that the fragmented political structure of the Miami area gave the
unwarranted appearance of low police expenditures in the city, since some
services may have been provided by overlapping districts. Analysis of the
overall situation and of the city's police expenditures levels at the end of the
decade (in Chapter 7) will provide a better perspective on this matter and on the
involvement of Hispanic groups (45 percent of the city's 1970 population) in
police administration and police/community relations.

Atlanta

The Context

In 1970 Atlanta's population of 495,000 was about 51 percent black and
about 1 percent Hispanic. Revenues, which would grow enormously during the
decade, were $198 per capita in 1970, not far from the mean for southern large
cities. Sixteen percent of Atlanta's population was below the poverty level, and
its ratio of black to white median income was 61 percent—low like the other
cities of the region. At 55 crimes per thousand in 1970, Atlanta was even then on
the high side for southern cities of 50,000 or more; their average crime rate at
the time was 33 crimes per thousand. However, Atlanta's 1971 expenditures for
police, at $32 per capita, while considerably greater than the $21 per capita
average for large southern cities, were still about $6 per capita under the level
expected given the city's crime rate, revenues, and demographic and economic
characteristics. Capital police expenditures at $3.50 per capita were about 50
cents per capita under the predicted value for the city.

Police Force: Discrimination in Hiring and Promotions

Newspaper reports early in the decade in Atlanta contain some discussion of
racial tension between blacks and the police, but very little in comparison to
other cities such as Chicago and Philadelphia, where blacks constituted sizable,
but less than majority proportions of the population. Relevant reporting in

Atlanta focused largely on the problems and issues relating to the underrepresentation of blacks on Atlanta's police force and their distribution throughout the ranks (cf. *Atlanta Journal,* 1/18/73, 7/19/73; for exceptions see 3/27/73, 12/7/73). That issue remained a problem throughout the decade. As Chapter 7 will detail, newspaper reporting on the subject was more extensive at the end of the decade than it was early on.

Police Expenditures and Black/White Control of the Police

Despite its location in the South, Atlanta had much in common with Detroit and Newark, majority black cities of the North: (1) its relative underfinancing of policing given the city's crime rate and socioeconomic characteristics, and (2) its public focus on black representation throughout the ranks of the police department. Outside of hiring and promotion, issues of dominance and control did not ostensibly influence policing appropriations or public police-related news discussion in Atlanta early in the 1970s. The demographic handwriting indicating the direction of political control was already on the wall.

Tulsa

The Context

Tulsa had a relatively small minority population in 1970: Blacks constituted only 10 percent of the population and Hispanics about 1 percent. A city of about 330,000 at that time, Tulsa had a crime rate of 38 per thousand, close to the average for cities over 50,000. Its ratio of black to white median income, at 49 percent, was considerably lower than the 1970 large city average of 67 percent. At $14 per capita, Tulsa's expenditures for policing in 1971 were about $8 per capita less than predicted on the basis of city characteristics and the crime rate; capital expenditures were very low at 25 cents per capita, about 75 cents per capita less than predicted.

Police Brutality toward Citizens

Some reporting throughout 1972 told of community demands for creation of a "Blue Ribbon Panel" of black and white citizens to investigate charges of police brutality during the arrests of three Northside Tulsans at the Gallery Supper Club (*Tulsa Daily World,* 9/4/72). The F.B.I. conducted an independent inquiry into the incident (*Oklahoma Eagle,* 9/7/72; *Tulsa Daily World,* 9/9/72), and there was a controversy over whether the Community Relations Commission panel investigating the incident should have subpoena powers to call unwilling witnesses (*Oklahoma Eagle,* 3/16/72).

Recruitment of Black Police Officers

Additional reporting discussed the need for more black police officers and the problems that black officers and their families faced within the black community given the poor image that police had among blacks (*Oklahoma Eagle,* 10/12/72). However, overall, there was not a great deal of press attention directed to problems of police/community relations in Tulsa, despite the city's location in the South. Tulsa's lower than expected level of expenditures for policing and the paucity of attention devoted to minority-related police issues in city newspapers both suggest that police/minority relations were not at the forefront of Tulsans' public concerns in 1972.

Location in the South: Summary and Overview

The South's historical bias toward blacks may help explain the intensity of reaction against blacks in Miami, despite the large proportion of Hispanics in the city. The situation in Atlanta was somewhat different. A majority black city, Atlanta (as was true of the other majority black cities we investigated) had an early 1970s' police/community focus on black representation on the police force despite the city's southern location. And in Tulsa, as in other cities with a small black population, some attention was devoted to the police brutality issue, but police/community relations did not assume a central place in the spectrum of public concerns.

The national study discussed earlier indicated that location in the South exacerbated the influence of percent black on public fiscal commitment to policing, but did not change the form of the impact (linear versus curvilinear). Regional location may similarly have influenced the police/community relations issues that were reported in local newspapers, by exacerbating white hostility toward a black minority, and intensifying black majority efforts for representation on the city police force.

WESTERN AND SOUTHWESTERN CITIES

Albuquerque

The Context

At $6.50 per capita, Albuquerque's reported level of capital police spending in 1971 was about six times greater than the mean for southern and western cities. It may be that special purchases or fiscal procedures accounted for the city's high level of capital spending in 1971, but as we will see in Chapter 7, capital police spending was still on the high side at the end of the decade. Blacks constituted just over 2 percent of the population in 1970. However, the fact that about 35 percent of Albuquerque's population was Hispanic suggests the importance of minority visibility and competition in 1971.

As a southwestern city with a large population (244,000 in 1970) and a relatively high 1970 crime rate (55 crimes per thousand) Albuquerque had a contextual and structural situation conducive to interaction among minority group threat, crime, and policing. The city's actual level of capital policing expenditures in 1970 exceeded the level predicted by our equation ($5.51 per capita), a disparity indicating that either the overall constellation of Albuquerque's traits or some elements not investigated in this study had boosted policing expenditures beyond expected levels. Whatever the trigger, high capital police spending in the city was persistent, remaining close to $2 per capita above the predicted level in 1978.

Police Brutality toward Citizens: Hispanics in the Forefront of Concern

Issues reported in Albuquerque newspapers in 1972 reflected some of the tensions suggested by the city's location on the threat curve. For example, there were several allegations of police brutality and harassment by both black and Chicano organizations. A report in the *Albuquerque Journal* (7/10/72) told of allegations by the city's black coalition that blacks were being harassed by stop and search police methods and that black cadets were being squeezed out of the police academy.

Earlier in 1972, a special commission had been appointed to investigate the killing of two members of the Brown Berets, a Mexican-American organization, allegedly by six police officers (*Albuquerque Journal*, 2/9/72). The men were shot—one nine times, the other six times—while allegedly taking dynamite from a construction site. One victim had a broken jaw and nose. Community members charged that the killing was designed to prevent the men's television appearance, scheduled for the next day, to publicize charges of police brutality in the prisons where these men had recently spent time. Additional charges that the men had been killed elsewhere and moved to the site, demolished during the incident's investigation, also appeared in the paper (*Albuquerque Journal*, 2/20/72). Later news reports (*Albuquerque Journal*, 3/9/72) indicated that a grand jury had exonerated the police officers, ruling the slayings justifiable. Further accounts described charges of jury bias and indicated that the jury was comprised primarily of Anglo residents of Albuquerque Heights (*Albuquerque Journal*, 3/11/72).

Mobilization of Police Resources

Some reporting focused directly on police funding efforts in Albuquerque. In May, for example, Police Chief Donald Byrd submitted a request for $2.9 million more than the $6.5 million allocated for the coming fiscal year, citing the need to keep the department up-to-date in light of the city's rising crime rate. Eighty-four percent of the requested increase would pay the salaries of 100 new police officers; 8.6 percent was slated for expenses; and 6.5 percent for property and equipment (*Albuquerque Journal*, 5/25/72). In addition, a $183,527 federal funding request designed to create a tactical squad and related departments within the Albuquerque Police Department was developed. Funds were requested to hire several attorneys for the tactical squad, three additional police officers, an analyst, patrol cars, radios, and surveillance equipment (*Albuquerque Journal,* 8/12/72).

Hispanic/Anglo Control over Policing Resources

In the early 1970s public attention in Albuquerque had begun to focus on issues relating to police brutality, especially toward Hispanics, and the city had begun to accelerate efforts to mobilize additional police resources. However, newspaper reports did not focus overtly on struggles between Hispanics and Anglos for control over police resources. Although both historical tradition and demography focused attention on Hispanics, the relative complacency of minority groups in the South, and the relative recency of national Hispanic political organization in the United States may have diluted these catalysts, thereby weakening Hispanic/Anglo struggles for control of police policy and resources.

Denver

The Context

Denver's Hispanic and black populations, at 17 percent and 9 percent, respectively in 1970, were sufficiently large to anticipate their visibility and threatening influence on the minority size/police resource relationship. Denver's population size (515,000 in 1970) and western location led to the expectation that the size of its Hispanic population, especially, would influence all categories of police expenditures, particularly in view of the city's high crime rate (74 per thousand) in 1970. Expectations are guarded, however, because 1971 police expenditures for salaries and operations were about $8 per capita less than predicted, and capital police expenditures (50 cents per capita) were also a bit under the predicted value.

Police Brutality toward Citizens

In view of the size of Denver's minority and total populations, it is no surprise that newspapers reported minority/police tension and conflict. Complaints by the Hispanic community were most prevalent, although there were some prominent anti-black incidents alleged. Newspaper accounts (*Denver Post,* 7/31/72) tell of charges of police harassment of Chicanos during a search for two youths alleged to have robbed a store; and of complaints over the closing of a park frequented by Hispanics after police were pelted and bombarded during a routine patrol call at the park (*Denver Post,* 8/1/72). Ongoing reporting from February through April describes the controversy over the clearing of patrol officers in the death of James Young, a former Black Panther leader, in a barrage of police shooting (*Denver Post,* 2/27/72, 3/5/72, 4/24/72).

A January article in the *Denver Post* (1/27/72) discussed two earlier investigations, conducted by a local consulting firm and an independent team of psychologists, of police relations with Denver's minority community. The first report suggested the establishment of a civilian advisory board to ensure minority participation; the second report recommended the formation of a panel of three persons—one selected by the police officer, one by the complainant, and the third by the two selected individuals—for use in cases where minority complaints against police are filed.

May reporting (*Denver Post*, 5/8/72) indicated that Police Chief George L. Seaton retired, citing ill health and family responsibilities as reasons, but amid speculation that pressure from minority, ethnic, and racial groups contributed to his decision. Acting Police Chief Arthur G. Dill replaced him in June, promising to continue Seaton's practice of bringing as many black and Hispanic police officers into the department as possible.

Police Force: Ethnic/Racial Bias in Hiring and Promotion

As late as August, however, Judge Alfred A. Arraj of the U.S. District Court threatened to impose sanctions against the Denver Civil Service Commission if greater efforts to recruit Hispanic and black policemen weren't forthcoming. Arraj charged that the city's policy of waiting for minority applicants to come to the police did not constitute affirmative action toward recruitment. The commission was required to report its progress every 15 days. In the judge's words, "It is time for the defendants to go to the mayor and other city officials and tell them about this court's order and get the necessary funds . . ." (*Denver Post*, 8/17/72). Follow-up reporting in August indicated that a new community committee had been formed to stimulate recruitment of minority firemen and policemen; the chair of the committee expressed his incredulity that there were only 41 blacks and 51 Chicanos in the 1250-member Denver Police Department (*Denver Post*, 8/23/72). The lack of high ranking black and Chicano officers in the police and fire departments was also noted in August reporting (*Denver Post*, 8/7/72).

Mobilization of Police Resources

Newspaper accounts during this period traced Denver's efforts to garner the necessary funds to increase its police spending levels, describe the city's application for some of LEAA's high impact anti-crime funds, and report that Denver was one of eight high crime rate cities to receive such funds (*Denver Post*, 1/14/72). Denver's portion amounted to $20 million over three years (*Denver Post*, 2/23/72). The program was planned to intensify current crime fighting methods without innovation; it was not intended to improve police/community relations (*Denver Post*, 1/16/72).

Given Denver's western location and the fact that its Hispanic population was almost twice the size of its black population, it is not surprising that police-related issues of minority/majority conflict focused more on Hispanics than on blacks. Anglos appeared to be in firm control of policing, studying, although still resisting, efforts to recruit Hispanic and black police officers and ensure minority participation in police policy making.

Sacramento

The Context

In 1970, Sacramento's population of 25,700 was 11 percent black and 13 percent Hispanic. Although the minority population was not large, it may have been noticeable in the aggregate. Actual policing expenditures totaled $36 per capita, $10 per capita greater than predicted. Expenditures for capital items, at $1 per capita, were about equal to the value predicted by our equation. Sacramento's 1970 crime rate of 46 per thousand was a bit above the large city average.

Police Force: Discrimination in Hiring and Promotions

Newspaper reporting in Sacramento discussed the charge by the Law Enforcement Association for Equality in April that minorities were excluded from appointment to the position of detective in the Sacramento Sheriff's Department (*Sacramento Bee,* 4/8/72). The president of the association indicated that there were no blacks and only two Mexican-Americans among the 79 appointees to the detective bureau. While the sheriff stated that he was not aware of any racial discrimination in his department, the State Fair Employment Practice Commission planned to investigate the situation.

Police Brutality toward Citizens

There were some allegations of brutality in 1972 reports (*Sacramento Bee,* 8/10/72; 12/30/72). One account with clear racial overtones involved the accidental killing of a 15-year-old youth after an erroneous police broadcast initiated a search for three black males leaving a bar. That incident led the Sacramento Police Officers' Association to raise the issue of limitations on police use of deadly force to life-threatening situations (*Sacramento Bee,* 12/30/72).

Minority Control of the Police

Although 24 percent of the Sacramento population was minority, its division into two fairly equally sized groups may have reduced its impact in terms of obtaining representation on the police force. While minority representation on the force and police/community relations were not major public issues in Sacramento, the news reports discussed above suggest that they were close to the arena of major public concerns.

San Francisco

The Context

Blacks and Hispanics together constituted about one-quarter of San Francisco's population of 716,000 in 1970 (about 12.5% each). There was also a sizeable Asian population in the city. Between 1964 and 1970 the city had had four riots and several protests. The city's police expenditures for salaries and operations, at $51 per capita, were considerably above the large city mean ($25 per capita), but still over $8 per capita less than predicted by our equations. Capital expenditures were about average for a large city, but again considerably below (more than $1 per capita) the predicted level.

Police Force: Discrimination in Recruitment and Promotions

Despite the four 1960s' riots, newspaper reporting in San Francisco in 1972 did not focus to any great degree on racial and ethnic tensions between police and the community. Some charges of racial bias in police work and recruiting surfaced. For example, when the residents of Potrero Hill, a predominantly black community, complained that police did not respond to their calls, and were less dilligent toward crime fighting than they were in other neighborhoods, the police chief sent squads of twenty-five men into the neighborhood to "protect" the residents. The officers (all white, since only white officers patrol the Hill), "frisked every person they came in contact with" (*Sun Reporter,* 9/9/72).

Earlier reports in April (*San Francisco Chronicle,* 4/29/72) cited the lack of black police cadets: Only seven of sixty were from racial minorities, and two of them were black. There were accounts in both April and July of efforts to recruit more black and Hispanic police officers. A July item (*San Francisco Chronicle,* 7/20/72) indicated that San Francisco had received special funds from the Bayview Model Cities Agency to recruit 20 black police officers, and cited Police Chief Donald Scott's promise that those who completed the training program would be guaranteed jobs on the force patrolling the entire city, not just its black residential areas.

Police Expenditures and Minority/Majority Control over the Police

As presented in the newspapers, the focus of minority efforts relating to the police was on representation by inclusion. Blacks and Hispanics had not begun to push for control over police policy or administration, as Detroit's blacks had, but they had begun to protest what they viewed as police bias and to demand more minority officers. The voices of Hispanic and Asian groups had not yet made it to San Francisco's newspapers. It is possible that here, as in Sacramento, the multifaceted composition of San Francisco's minority population reduced its impact in city politics overall, and on police force policy in particular.

Location in the West and Southwest: Summary and Overview

Overall, detailed analysis of individual cities in the West and Southwest further illustrates the impact of regional context and minority size on collective commitment to policing and on police/community relations. In Albuquerque, a southwestern city with a large Hispanic population, social control resource allocation was high early in the decade. News reporting revealed some evidence of Hispanic/police hostility. Denver, with a smaller Hispanic population and a noticeable black minority, had low levels of police spending early in the decade, but many newspaper articles indicated problems of minority representation on the police force and cited specific allegations of police brutality toward Hispanics, and (to a lesser degree) toward blacks. In San Francisco, the mix of ethnic groups was extensive; blacks and Hispanics had begun to call for more representation on the police force, but neither group made noticeable progress toward influence over police policy. Finally, in Sacramento, the 24 percent minority population in the city was fairly evenly divided between blacks and Hispanics (although the division was slanted toward Hispanics). It may be that this fragmentation of the minority population reduced the threat engendered by the group, and prevented the interests of either blacks or Hispanics from becoming paramount.

REGION, MINORITY GROUP THREAT, AND SOCIAL CONTROL: DISCUSSION AND CONCLUSIONS

Quantitative evidence provided by the national analysis of the determinants of municipal police expenditure levels suggests that region, as a sociohistorical construct influencing the relationships between racial and ethnic groups, is a filter through which minority groups are viewed and is thereby important in determining the level of threat engendered by racial and ethnic minorities. For both black and Hispanic populations the impact of minority size on public fiscal commitment to policing is greater, even after controls for regional socioeconomic variations, in those regions where the minority group's history of interaction with whites has been characterized by greatest tension and conflict.

While the perspective provided by region influences the impact of minority size on social control resource determination, other realities of regional differentiation provide for variations in crime rates that are especially reflected in violent crime levels. Since fear of crime is influenced by both minority group threat and actual crime levels, the accumulation of regional variations in perceived minority threat and in crime rates is cause for concern. This is especially relevant in a decade that witnessed the resurgence of public expression of racial and ethnic animosities, and in a nation that had turned away from problems of poverty and minority entitlement, focusing instead on problems of national prosperity and the accumulation of individual wealth.

Detailed analyses of individual cities, all from regions with long historical traditions of tense relationships between whites and the prevailing minority group, illustrate the impact of regional history and population composition on police/community relations. Problems of minority representation on the police force, allegations of racially or ethnically directed brutality by police officers, complaints of slow response time, or neglect of the policing needs of minority communities begin the litany of tensions surrounding policing as it relates to minority communities. Add to them a long history of intergroup hostility and discrimination and the stage is set for (1) excesses in police use of deadly force [found by Liska and Yu (1987) to occur with greatest frequency when police face potentially violent situations in largely black communities], and (2) labeling to influence routine police activity, encouraging the "aggressive preventive patrolling" seen as repressive by members of minority communities.

The individual city vignettes stimulate thought in other directions as well. It may be true, for example, that a large multifaceted minority population, such as was characteristic of San Francisco, Sacramento, and Denver in 1970, does not constitute a strong enough political force to influence police/community relations in general or to secure significant representation on the police force. A multifaceted group may also not be as visible as is a homogeneous minority population, thereby engendering less threat. It may also be true that an individual minority group is not perceived as a clear threat to the majority population unless it constitutes approximately 20 percent or more of the population. A large minority population, divided by ethnicity and race, may simply be too amorphous to be perceived as a threat, and too divided to represent a significant political force.

The next three chapters explore these and other issues in assessing the changes that occurred in U.S. cities during the 1970s. The influence of time and distance from the racial strife that ushered in the decade would seem to cut across all the relationships we have been examining and affect the link between the relative size of a minority group and the level of perceived minority group threat, as well as their impact on public fiscal commitment to policing. Chapter 5 begins investigation of the influence of the decade's transitions on social control resource allocation and on police/community relations with study of the changes that occurred in five of the major industrial centers in our group of case studies.

5

The Changing National Perspective: A Decade of Transition in Large Industrial Cities

Nationwide the 1970s witnessed a reduction in the level of concern about interracial crisis resolution in U.S. cities and an increase in concern about Hispanic Americans. At approximately the same time in the realm of scholarship, study of police resource determination demonstrated the influence of stratification and the distribution of power on collective commitment to social control. A new understanding of the police emerged, casting the municipal force as a political resource supported by groups of established position and power, and resented or, at best, viewed as irrelevant by those lacking traditional resources. As discussed in Chapter 1, new theories explaining collective commitment to social control added racial, ethnic, and economic stratification to a model that had been based largely on municipal revenues, crime, population size, and density.

The new model has not been tested with post-1971 data, however. Since the pattern of racial and ethnic relations characteristic of the early 1970s had changed by the end of the decade, comparison of the impact of race and ethnicity on municipal police resource determination at these two time periods provides a good test of the revised model. This chapter compares cross-sectional analyses of the determinants of municipal police resources in 1971 and 1978. Central to this test are propositions relating the influence of social context to the link between minority population composition and the level of public commitment to social control. Special attention is devoted to the impact of the size of the black and Hispanic populations on the level of policing expenditures in different regions and city size groups of the United States.

SHIFTING NATIONAL PRIORITIES

Recent evidence indicates that by 1972, Nixon administration officials believed that the threat of large-scale black rioting had passed. As Button (1978: 151) has noted, for the first time since its inception in 1969 the "LEAA [Law Enforcement Assistance Administration] Annual Report of allocations of state action funds for fiscal 1973 showed no categorical listing of expenditures for civil disorders and riot control." For the four preceding years significant funds had been allocated in that category.

Also indicative of this trend was the demise of the Community Relations Service (CRS), a federal organization within the Bureau of Justice. The CRS had focused its late 1960s' efforts on the resolution of community racial conflicts. In 1973, however, its staff was reduced by two-thirds and its funding was cut by approximately one-half, signaling the Nixon administration's recognition of the easing of racial tensions. At this point the activities of the agency focused on interracial crisis resolution (rather than on prevention) and, increasingly, on other "'emerging' minorities such as American Indians, Asian Americans, Mexican-Americans and Eskimos" (Button, 1978: 151; cf. also annual report of the Community Relations Service, 1973:3, 1974:6). Furthermore, the F.B.I.'s 1974 annual report indicates a similar shift in its ten-year-old view that blacks were the most serious threat to internal stability (F.B.I., 1974: 14-17; Button, 1978: 151).

As the focus of federal attention shifted from blacks to other minorities, and from issues of law and order to other concerns, it is possible that local attention had new priorities as well. In some regions Hispanics may have triggered a greater degree of threat than blacks, given the rapid influx of Cubans and increased national focus on the "problem" of illegal aliens and the integrity of the Mexican-American border. The simultaneous reduction in national fear of violent racial confrontations may have led to a redirection of police resource mobilization—away from the capital acquisitions characteristic of the post-riot period and toward bolstering the level and training of personnel.

Comparison of beginning- and end-of-the-decade data permits investigation of the extent to which changes in the federal focus influenced local priorities. The riots and protests of the 1960s did not extend very far into the 1970s. The generally calm racial climate of the seventies could have turned public attention away from social control issues, thereby reducing the impact of minority size on all categories of policing expenditures. This change would be most evident for capital policing expenditures, given the shift in the focus of LEAA funding efforts by the end of the decade, and the reduction in federal attention to law and order. Discussion now turns to the evidence.

THE NATIONAL ANALYSIS

By 1978 the pattern of results described in earlier chapters had changed in several important respects (see Tables A.2-A.10, and Tables 5.1-5.6). First, for

Table 5.1
Significant Predictors of Total Municipal Police Expenditures,
Cities ≥ 50,000 Population, 1978

```
CITY CRIME RATE        (+)

CITY REVENUES          (+)

POPULATION DENSITY     (+)

PERCENT BLACK          (+)

PERCENT POOR           (-)
```

```
EXPLANATORY POWER OF FULL EQUATION   47%
```

Table 5.2
Significant Predictors of Capital Police Expenditures,
Cities ≥ 50,000 Population, 1978

```
POPULATION DENSITY          (-)

INTER-RACIAL INEQUALITY     (+)

CITY CRIME RATE             (+)
```

```
EXPLANATORY POWER OF FULL EQUATION   5%
```

Table 5.3
Significant Predictors of Total Municipal Police Expenditures,
Southern Cities ≥ 50,000 Population, 1978

```
CITY CRIME RATE        (+)

POPULATION DENSITY     (+)

PER CENT BLACK         (+)

PER CENT POOR          (-)

POPULATION SIZE        (+)
```

```
EXPLANATORY POWER OF FULL EQUATION   64%
```

Table 5.4
Significant Predictors of Capital Police Expenditures,
Southern Cities ≥ 50,000 Population, 1978

PER CENT BLACK   (+)

EXPLANATORY POWER OF FULL EQUATION   6%

Table 5.5
Significant Predictors of Total Municipal Police Expenditures,
Southern and Western Cities, 1978

PER CENT HISPANIC   (∿)*

CITY CRIME RATE   (+)

CITY REVENUE   (+)

POPULATION SIZE   (+)

PERCENT POOR   (-)

POPULATION DENSITY   (+)

PERCENT BLACK   (+)

EXPLANATORY POWER OF FULL EQUATION   49%

*(∿) CURVILINEAR RELATIONSHIP

Table 5.6
Significant Predictors of Capital Police Expenditures,
Southern and Western Cities, 1978

NONE

EXPLANATORY POWER OF FULL EQUATION   1%

all cities and for the large and small city subpopulations, the model based on city sociodemographic characteristics and the crime rate was no longer as effective in explaining municipal police expenditures. For example, in large cities about 47 percent of the variance in police salaries and operations was explained by the equation in 1978, 23 percent less than in 1976. For capital expenditures the model explained only 5 percent of the variance in 1978, 16 percent less than in 1971.

This explanatory deficit in 1978 crosscuts the contextual divisions that emerged as important demarcators in the analysis of the allocation of 1971 social control resources: (1) In large cities, the model explained 23 percent less variance in total municipal police expenditures in 1978, and 17 percent less in capital expenditures; (2) in southern and western cities, it explained 24 percent less variance in total expenditures and 20 percent less in capital expenditures; (3) in large southern cities, the explanatory deficit was smaller in 1978, only 6 percent, for total expenditures, but it was about 35 percent for capital expenditures. For southern small cities, the 1978 explanatory deficits are 13 percent and 20 percent, respectively.

The pattern of findings suggests that by 1978 in all city subgroups the climate determining the collective commitment to social control had changed. The determinants of police expenditures at the end of the decade were not as consistent across cities as they were in 1971. The decline in federal allocations for law and order may well have contributed to this trend. Some important determinants of all categories of 1978 policing expenditures in cities may not be included in the model, or the set of predictors may not have been as consistent as in 1971.

Outside of southern large cities, where the model developed to explain 1971 police expenditures largely holds its own in 1978, the weakened effectiveness of the model's explanatory power may be due to reductions in the economic and political distance between dominant and subordinate groups and to the decline in federal allocations for law and order. Both trends would have permitted greater variability in the determinants of police funding.

The economic distance between blacks and whites at the end of the decade remained greatest in southern cities (where blacks were earning on average only about 60% of whites' income in contrast to about 70% elsewhere). It is possible that the continued economic polarization between the races in the South accounted for the lasting effectiveness of the 1971 model in explaining 1978 municipal police expenditures in southern cities.

Also indicative of the importance of interracial competition in determining local levels of law enforcement resources is the significance of the ratio of black/white median income as a positive, significant predictor of capital policing expenditures in 1978 in the national group of cities and in the large city subpopulation. By the end of the decade, cities outside of the South spent more on capital police items where black economic competition was becoming a reality. This was not the case in 1971, when the effect of interracial income inequality was insignificant.

In addition, in the large city model for 1978 (shown in Tables 5.1 and 5.2 and in Table A.3), while percent black retained its significant influence on total police expenditures and those for police salaries and operations, the threat curve characteristic of the 1971 percent black/capital expenditures relationship was not evident. One interpretation of these findings is that by 1978 capital police resources were not being mobilized in response to a black threat; that the shift in LEAA, F.B.I., and presidential priorities from blacks to other "emerging minorities" was reflected at the local level. Toward the end of the decade it appears that the threat posed by blacks may have become centered on economic competition, while the threat was more vague and generalized earlier in the decade, responding simply to the relative size of the black population through mobilization of capital policing resources as if in preparation for escalation of conflict.

Further evidence of the influence of social context on the relationship between minority group threat, crime, and policing is found in the South (see Tables 5.3 and 5.4 and Table A.5). In southern large cities percent black continued to influence capital police expenditures in 1978, but the threat curve evident in 1971 was no longer apparent. Thus, the national relaxation of concern about a black threat had some effect on municipal police expenditures in the South despite the region's heritage of tense black/white relations and the continued high prediction power of the 1971 police expenditures model. In southern small cities, the impact of black visibility on collective commitment to social control remained insignificant in 1978 as it was early in the decade, reinforcing the importance of the small/large city differences in anonymity and informal social control (see Table A.6).

The Emerging Hispanic Threat

Members of "emerging minorities," to use the federal administration's lexicon for Hispanic population groups—Mexican-Americans, Cubans, Puerto Ricans, Haitians, and others of Central American and Latin American origin—merited more attention at the local level and had a greater impact on municipalities' collective commitment to social control in 1978 than they did earlier in the decade. Nationally, the relative size of Hispanic groups as a percentage of city populations had increased from about 6.9 percent to 8.2 percent during the decade, but the regional distribution of Hispanics remained largely the same. The proportion Hispanic grew in southern and western cities from 10.2 percent to 11.8 percent and in the northeastern/northcentral city sub-population from 2.9 percent to 4 percent.

Since the overall size of the Hispanic population was increasing and receiving much national attention during the decade, it is not surprising that the impact of percent Hispanic on policing resources was greater toward the end of the decade than at the beginning. The influence of the size of the Hispanic population was greatest in those regions with a sociohistorical tradition of tension between Hispanic-related groups and non-Hispanics.

By 1978 the Hispanic threat had assumed national dimensions, and the threat curve for the salaries/operations category of police expenditures mirrored the curve found for blacks earlier in the decade (see Table A.8). Again, not surprisingly, while the impact of percent Hispanic on collective commitment to social control was significant in cities of the South and West, it was still not statistically significant in northern and north central cities (see Tables A.9 and A.10, and Table 5.5).

These results generally confirm the 1971 findings. The data also indicate that the relative impact of percent Hispanic on social control resources was greater in 1978 than in 1971 (see the regression coefficients in Table A.9). For the national population of cities and for both regional subgroups, the threat curve noted in the relationship between 1971 capital policing expenditures and percent Hispanic was not apparent in the 1978 data, suggesting the importance of LEAA in stimulating capital policing expenditures in the early part of the decade. Of interest, however, is the impact of percent Hispanic on total police expenditures and on its subdivision expenditures for salaries and operations: It was significant and curvilinear in the national population of cities and in the southern and western city subgroups in 1978. The regression coefficients indicate the same general pattern as in 1971, but with greater intensity (sufficient for statistical significance). Plotted in Figure 5.1, the curve is similar to the threat curve found for capital police expenditures early in the decade, except that it begins to decline a bit before the 40 percent point where the 1971 capital expenditures curve began its descent. Toward the end of the decade, then, the level of personnel expenditures responded positively and in a non-linear manner to the

Figure 5.1
Relationship between 1978 Expenditures for Police Salaries and Operations and Percent Hispanic in Southern and Western Cities (N=301)

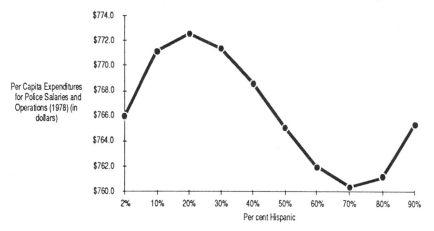

Note: $\hat{Y}^* = .73027X - .02349X^2 + .00017X^3$.

* The values plotted include the sum of the constant term and the means of the independent variables in the estimating equation.

size of the Hispanic population (possibly resulting in the hiring of more police officers), dropping off after Hispanics constituted more than one-third of the population.

CITY ILLUSTRATIONS OF THE DECADE'S CHANGES

The updated city vignettes begun in previous chapters illustrate national and local changes in the law enforcement climate and focus. As Table 2.8 indicates, the cities we have considered varied in their level of spending in 1978. Some, like Philadelphia and Albuquerque, were high spenders in 1978. Others, such as Sacramento, San Francisco, Minneapolis, Wichita, and Miami, were at the lower end of the spending continuum, as they had been in 1971. In the following pages for all these cities, we will use newspaper analysis to try to assess the growth or decline of minority threat within them, investigating the changes wrought by the 1970s. In this chapter we focus on five large industrial cities: Detroit, Philadelphia, Baltimore, Chicago, and Newark. Chapters 6 and 7 update mid-sized cities and cities of the South and West.

Detroit

The Context

By 1980, the crime rate in Detroit had risen to about 106 crimes per thousand population, still higher than average for cities of 50,000 or more, but not as high proportionately as it had been in 1970 (see Table 5.7). Like many other large cities, Detroit was smaller in both population size and density in 1980 than it had been in 1970. The city's revenue base had improved over the decade; at $1078 per capita, it was about twice the large city average in 1980. However, 19 percent of city residents were poor, almost double the average for large cities, and two-thirds of city residents were minority individuals (63% black and 2.4% Hispanic). The ratio of black to white median income was about the same in 1980 as it was in 1970 (0.79).

Reported police expenditures for salaries and operations, at $126 per capita in 1978, were high overall, about $54 per capita greater than predicted by the city's sociodemographic characteristics. Capital expenditures, while high at $3.70 per capita, were only about 60 cents per capita higher than predicted. They were soon to be cut drastically, however, in an austerity program that was not unrelated to a reevaluation of the role and importance of policing by the new black majority in the city. Police-related reporting in the city's newspapers provides the details.

Progress in Police/Community Relations

Much 1979 to 1980 newspaper reporting in Detroit reflected the history of police/community relations in the city. Articles entitled "Detroit Police: The Long March from 1976" (*Detroit Free Press,* 11/25/79), "How Tough Precinct

Table 5.7
Detroit Profile

Characteristic	1970	1980
Population Size	1511 thsnd	1203 thsnd
Population Density	10949 sqmi	8874 sqmi
Per Capita Revenue	$272	$1078
Per Cent Poor	11%	19%
Per Cent Black	44%	63%
Per Cent Hispanic	1.8%	2.4%
Black/White Median Income	.78	.79
Crime Rate Per Thousand	84	106
Police Expenditures Per Capita		
Total	$54	$129
Salaries/Operations	$53	$126
Capital	$1.2	$3.7

was Turned Around" (*Detroit Free Press,* 8/10/80), and "City Police: A Past of Racism, Brutality?" (*Detroit Free Press,* 12/7/80) discussed reductions in police brutality and improved police/community relations over the decade. One article in the *Detroit Free Press* (8/31/80) cited Mayor Coleman Young's 1973 campaign promise "to end police brutality against blacks, and to hire more minority police officers to make the Department reflect the city's new black majority." Young had his work cut out for him; news reporting alludes to his six-year struggle with two police unions and with the department's own power structure—a struggle that produced visible progress, but not complete success.

Civilian Board of Police Commissioners

Although voters in 1973 had also approved a change in the city charter replacing the single commissioner with a board consisting of five civilians, language in union contracts slowed the board's attempt to control the citizen complaint process (*Detroit Free Press,* 8/31/80). By 1979, however, Detroit Police Chief William Hart described the 30-year old black woman then heading the city's Civilian Board of Police Commissioners as "an outstanding symbol of what the commission was meant to be," indicating further that "there is good cooperation between the commission and the office of the chief" (*Detroit Free Press* 1/22/79). Another article (*Detroit Free Press,* 8/31/80), headlined "Six Years After Its Inception, Review Board Fulfills Its Mandate," gave the board significant credit for improving police/community relations, "adoption of an affirmative action program and the hiring and promotion of blacks to achieve a better racial balance."

Police Layoffs: Recognition That Police Cannot Reduce Crime

The sense of progress in police/community relations (including greater representation of blacks on the police force) reflected in news reporting was one of three major themes in the end-of-the-decade reporting. A second major theme was the emergence of a general recognition that increasing the number of police officers was not an effective antidote to crime. "Programs, Not Police, Called Curb For Crime" (*Detroit Free Press,* 6/24/79) described comments by a Detroit Democrat, U.S. Representative John Conyers, at the annual meeting of the National Organization of Black Law Enforcement Officers. Representative Conyers and the organization's leaders "called . . . for more programs to deal with social problems rather than more police officers to combat crime."

Almost a year and a half later, the *Detroit Free Press* (11/10/80) announced "Police Doing Well In Spite Of Layoffs," and explained that the increased efficiency and experience of the smaller police force after the 690-officer layoff in early September had helped contain crime and prevent erosion of police services. The acceptance of the reduced size of the police force came in the midst of two years of reporting relating to a serious budget deficit in the city and Mayor Young's plans to lay off about 700 police officers in order to meet city spending limitations. Reporting stressed the adverse consequences of the layoffs in terms of the city's affirmative action program, and threats of job actions by the city's police union.

Crackdown on Police Misconduct and Brutality

In the midst of Detroit's budgetary worries and the positive reflection of improved police/community relations, the third prominent theme in the city's end-of-the-decade reporting was the continued efforts to "crackdown" (*Detroit Free Press,* 5/9/80) on police misconduct and brutality, with emphasis on their cost to the taxpayer. "Police Brutality, Misconduct Cases Cost Millions," was the announcement in the *Detroit Free Press* (8/3/80) in August 1980. Reporting cited the expense to the taxpayer of lawsuits against police officers, indicating that Detroit City Council members urged "stricter internal Police Department controls as part of a program to cut down lawsuit settlements against the city" (*Detroit Free Press,* 5/9/80).

Detroit in Retrospect

Overall, the seventies was a decade of major change in the relationship between police and community in Detroit: (1) As the city's demographic profile changed, tipping the balance to majority black, city residents assumed greater control over the police, especially over citizen complaint procedures. (2) The perceived value of police officers in terms of citizen safety and the overall crime rate was being recalculated and reduced in light of the city's budget deficit. These deficits forced a valuation of city priorities, and police force strength was not as high on the list as it had once been. Detroit also had to cut spending in other areas, but as earlier research indicates, even the most fiscally stressed cities ignore other budget priorities to provide for high police expenditures when the minority/majority struggle for dominance has not been resolved. All evidence—both the cutbacks in police appropriations and the issues raised in the press—suggests that intergroup competition for political control of the city had been resolved in Detroit by the end of the decade. Blacks had the upper hand, and scaled back police resources in light of their recognition of the limitations of police work in reducing crime.

Philadelphia

The Context

Not surprisingly, Philadelphia's population declined in both size and density during the decade; the percentage of city residents below the poverty level increased from 11 percent to 17 percent, and the percentage of blacks in the population increased by 4 percent to 38 percent (see Table 5.8). Hispanics constituted 3.8 percent of the population, up from 1.4 percent in 1970. A sign of the decade's national economic polarization between rich and poor in cities, the ratio of black to white median income declined nine percentage points, with Philadelphia blacks earning on average only 63 percent of whites' income in 1980.

The city's reported rate of total index crimes, at 60 per thousand, was less than the 81 per thousand 1980 average for large cities. Police expenditures in 1978, on the other hand, approximately $188 per capita for salaries and operations,

Table 5.8
Philadelphia Profile

Characteristic	1970	1980
Population Size	1950 thsnd	1688 thsnd
Population Density	15109 sqmi	12413 sqmi
Per Capita Revenue	$363	$927
Per Cent Poor	11%	17%
Per Cent Black	34%	38%
Per Cent Hispanic	1.4%	3.8%
Black/White Median Income	.72	.63
Crime Rate Per Thousand	23	60
Police Expenditures Per Capita		
Total	$60	$190
Salaries/Operations	$58	$188
Capital	$2.2	$1.9

were much greater (by \$125 per capita) than predicted on the basis of the city's socioeconomic characteristics. Capital expenditures also remained slightly above average (40 cents per capita) in 1978, although to a lesser degree than earlier in the decade (when they were 60 cents per capita over the predicted level).

Police/Community Relations: New Beginnings

Newspaper reporting in Philadelphia at the end of the decade reflected the legacy of Frank L. Rizzo's years as police commissioner and mayor, and described the new course charted by his successor as mayor, William J. Green, and the new police commissioner, Morton B. Solomon. The change of atmosphere, expectations, and rules relating to police use of deadly force was both evident and necessary in light of the U.S. Justice Department's suit alleging police abuse on the part of the Philadelphia Police Department.

U.S. Justice Department Lawsuit

During the last year of Frank Rizzo's administration the U.S. Civil Rights Commission held hearings on allegations of police brutality involving 22 Philadelphia police officers (*Evening Bulletin*, 2/26/79). On August 13, the U.S. Justice Department filed suit against the Philadelphia Police Department charging it with "systematic abuses of citizens which are 'shocking to the conscience'" (*Evening Bulletin*, 8/13/79). Drew Days, chief of the Civil Rights Division of the Justice Department, was quoted in the *Evening Bulletin* (8/13/79) as indicating that "It's the first time the Federal Government has ever gone after a police department as an institution . . . Our desire . . . is to get at what we see as a system, a system that condones and perpetuates police brutality. We're going into this suit challenging official practices. We're not trying to get an individual."

Named in the suit were Mayor Rizzo and 18 top city and police officials along with Police Commissioner O'Neill, the prisons superintendent, and the city's medical examiner among others. The suit alleged that:

illegal practices have been implemented by the defendants and their agents and their employees in the Philadelphia Police Department (PPD) and have deprived persons of all races, colors, and national origins of basic federal rights. Such practices have been implemented with the intent, and/or the effect of inflicting disproportionate abuse upon black persons and persons of Hispanic origin . . . (*Philadelphia Inquirer*, 8/19/79).

Mayor Rizzo dismissed the federal suit as "hogwash"; at a press conference he and Police Commissioner Joseph F. O'Neill indicated that they "do not believe police brutality is widespread, if it exists at all, in the 8,000 member Police Department" (*Evening Bulletin*, 8/14/79). The suit asked for a cutoff of federal funds (about \$4 million a year) (*Washington Post*, 8/14/79) to the police department if it did not correct abuses, and sought an injunction to halt the Rizzo administration's alleged acquiescence of police abuse. The suit also alleged that "investigations within the Police Department of brutality complaints are conducted in a manner to exonerate accused officers" (*Evening Bulletin*, 8/14/79).

Reporting recounted the history of "the last time Philadelphia officials were charged with condoning police brutality" (in 1972) when "U.S. District Court Judge John P. Fullam ordered the Police Department to set up a program to improve the handling of citizen complaints, but Fullam later was overruled by the Supreme Court, which held that the federal courts had no authority to interfere in the running of local police departments . . . [and that the] case failed to show a widespread pattern of police abuse" (*Evening Bulletin*, 8/14/79).

Mayor Rizzo, police commissioner in Philadelphia from 1967 to 1971, was alleged to have initiated many of the illegal policies and to have perpetuated them as mayor. After denying the charges in the suit as "hogwash" (*Evening Bulletin*, 8/14/79), Rizzo told a television audience that the PPD was "strong enough to invade Cuba and win . . ." (*Evening Bulletin*, 8/20/79). In his words, Philadelphia police were "the toughest cops in the world" (*Washington Post*, 8/14/79).

City officials sought dismissal of the lawsuit on the grounds that it lacked substance, calling it a " 'vile' attack upon the integrity of the city of Philadelphia and every police officer," and indicating that the policies, practices, and procedures of the City had been "attacked by the government of the United States" in what State Representative Dennis O'Brien referred to as "a blanket indictment" of the 8000 members of Philadelphia's force (*Evening Bulletin*, 9/5/79).

Dismissal of Charges

In October, U.S. District Court Judge J. William Ditter, Jr., dismissed most of the U.S. Justice Department's police abuse suit (*Evening Bulletin*, 10/31/79), citing its careful cultivation via the press and the timing of the suit (such that neither the outgoing mayor nor the outgoing police commissioner would be able to defend themselves before trial proceedings) as evidence of bias on the part of the Justice Department. The remainder of the charges were dismissed less than two months later (*Evening Bulletin*, 12/14/79).

The U.S. Justice Department did not leave the issue there, however. Even after the election of Mayor Green and Morton B. Solomon's assumption of the office of police commissioner, the justice department initiated an appeal of the dismissal (*Evening Bulletin*, 2/26/80).

Police Use of Deadly Force Curtailed

Reporting throughout 1980 clearly indicated that Mayor Green and Commissioner Solomon were beginning a major effort to revamp the image, environment, and culture of the PPD. First, on April 30, Solomon issued guidelines on police use of deadly force (*Evening Bulletin, 9/2/80*), and made it clear that he would not continue the practice of his predecessors, Rizzo and O'Neill, in retaining officers who made a mistake with good intentions. "Under Commissioner, Police 'Walk the Line,'" headlined one article in the *Evening Bulletin* (9/2/80). Another, in the *Philadelphia Inquirer* (1/13/80), quipped, "At the Police Department, A New Broom Sweeps Fast." Further reporting announced that the "winds of change are blowing through the Philadelphia Police Department on the sensitive issues of brutality and abuse of authority, but so far only gentle breezes have reached the public" (*Evening Bulletin, 1/17/80*). Second, Police Commissioner Solomon established a plan to first use training, then discipline, to control verbal abuse and excessive use of force, and to respond to instances of outright brutality with arrest, as with any crime (*Evening Bulletin, 1/17/80*).

A third and related initiative in the effort to reduce brutality and improve the image of the PPD was the issuance of clear rules for police use of deadly force, enunciated on a wallet card carried by all officers. It was reported that these rules were designed to prevent police from unhostering firearms unless a life was in danger or it was necessary to prevent the escape of someone believed to have committed a felony (*Philadelphia Inquirer, 4/20/80*). The announcement was accompanied by a stern warning that those who violated the deadly force rules would be disciplined publicly, a change in practice that led to protest on the part of some officers (*Philadelphia Inquirer, 10/19/80*). The *Philadelphia Inquirer* (10/19/80) greeted the policy as a welcome "180 degree change" in direction, noting that "for the first time in years police officers are being fired for making serious errors in judgment or overreacting in the line of duty."

Although instances of excessive use of force did not come to a complete halt, they were dealt with swiftly and severely. The 1980 shooting death of a 17-year-old youth by a Philadelphia policeman, for example, resulted in the officer's suspension and a charge of murder (*Evening Bulletin, 8/31/80*). The incident, involving a car chase with the youth driving a stolen car, touched off three consecutive nights of violence in North Philadelphia. Crowds of blacks took to the streets in protest, alleging that the 14-year veteran officer beat the youth with a revolver and shot him in "cold blood" (*Evening Bulletin, 8/31/80*). Newspaper reporting on the subject pointed out the speed with which the officer was suspended and charged under the new guidelines (*Evening Bulletin, 8/31/80; 8/26/80*).

Police Layoffs: Recognition That Police Cannot Reduce Crime

As efforts were being made to increase police accountability, reductions in the number of officers began, leading to a decline in their number from 8079 to 7395, in a force that "had been virtually immune to such cutbacks under Rizzo and O'Neill" (*Evening Bulletin, 9/2/80*). It may be that this was the result not only of the fiscal exigencies of metropolitan centers in the early 1980s, but also of a general revaluation of the importance of police in controlling crime.

An article in the *Evening Bulletin* (2/16/80) during the layoffs gave credence

to this view, proclaiming that "police size has no effect on crime rate . . . ,"
and introducing a report by the Citizens Crime Commission of Philadelphia on
the crime statistics of the 12 largest American cities. The report "also concluded
that in the 20-year period from 1958 to 1978, Philadelphia added more police
manpower, proportionately, than any other old-line, industrial city of the East
and Midwest included in the study, increasing police force size by about 63
percent in contrast to Chicago's 41 percent, Baltimore's 28 percent, New York's
19 percent, and Boston's decrease of 3.3 percent.

A later article (*Evening Bulletin*, 3/18/80) indicated that during this time
Philadelphia's population size decreased by about 14 percent, and speculated
that the changing demographic composition of Philadelphia—with older citizens
replacing young people—would lead to a reduction of crime, since younger
people commit more crimes. That and the decline in overall population of the
city were expected to result in a decrease in both the crime rate and the need for
police.

Philadelphia in Retrospect

Like other northeastern industrial cities, Philadelphia declined in population
and increased in minority composition during the 1970s. The economic
bifurcation of the city's blacks and whites also increased, as did its level of
poverty. Yet police expenditures at the end of the decade remained noticeably
above both the large city average and the levels expected on the basis of the
city's crime rate and socioeconomic characteristics. However, considerable
evidence suggests a change in the upward climbing trajectory of hostile
police/minority relations in Philadelphia by the end of the decade. Curbs were
placed on police use of deadly force, and new standards requiring greater police
officer discipline and cracking down on both verbal and physical brutality were
enforced.

Greater recognition of the limitations of police officers in curbing crime also
was apparent in reported public discussion of policing. It could be argued that
such talk served merely as rationalization for necessary police layoffs resulting
from the declining economic circumstances of some sectors of the city's
population. However, the fact that city revenues remained high and that police
appropriations had never been questioned under the previous "law and order"
city administration gives credibility to the interpretation that the winds had
begun to shift from law and order toward police accountability with greater
understanding of the broad contextual determinants of crime.

Baltimore

The Context

By 1980, Baltimore's population had declined by about 120,000 to 787,000
(see Table 5.9). City revenues, at $1678 per capita in 1980, were considerably
above the large city average, but in light of the city's 19 percent poor, were

Table 5.9
Baltimore Profile

Characteristic	1970	1980
Population Size	906 thsnd	787 thsnd
Population Density	11615 sqmi	9798 sqmi
Per Capita Revenue	$618	$1678
Per Cent Poor	14%	19%
Per Cent Black	46%	55%
Per Cent Hispanic	1%	1%
Black/White Median Income	.74	.66
Crime Rate Per Thousand	69	97
Police Expenditures Per Capita		
Total	$67	$89
Salaries/Operations	$58	$89
Capital	$9.2	$.65

probably insufficient to provide all the necessary social services. Crime also increased, from 69 to 97 crimes per thousand, keeping Baltimore's crime rate above the national average for large cities, but not excessively so. Reported overall police expenditures in Baltimore remained greater than expected in 1978, by about $6 per capita, but all of the excess was in salaries and operations. Capital police expenditures plummeted from $9 per capita in 1971 to about 65 cents per capita in 1978, about $2 per capita less than expected.

Baltimore became a majority black city during this decade. The 1980 population of the city was 55 percent black, up 9 percentage points from the beginning of the decade. Inequality between black and white city residents had increased over the decade with blacks earning, on average, only 66 percent of whites' median income in 1980, as opposed to 74 percent in 1970.

Police Layoffs: A Result of Union Busting and Reduced
Municipal Law and Order Appropriations

Reports in Baltimore's newspapers throughout 1979 focus on problems of police staffing and salary issues. The Baltimore *Sun* (2/14/79) reported that although the Baltimore Police Department was "authorized to carry 3,337 sworn personnel . . . [the] intermittent hiring freeze and the higher-than-usual attrition rate [due to low salaries] had decreased the strength of the Department to 2,975." Police Commissioner Pomerleau is quoted as having "informed city officials that the department will be at the dangerously low level it was in 1966 [when there were approximately 3000 police officers] unless additional officers are hired."

Two months later, the state legislature did not approve the city's request for a $3.3 million financial aid package designed to increase the pay of city police, alleged by the local chapter of the Fraternal Order of Police to be below competitive levels. Representatives of the F.O.P. were scheduled to meet with Mayor Schaefer to discuss the problem, "the first time that a labor organization representing police officers has sought to discuss wages with the city since an illegal police strike in 1974, when scores of officers were fired and the police union ousted" (*Sun*, 4/13/79).

Reporting in May (*Sun*, 5/4/79) indicated that Mayor Schaefer had budgeted $2.7 million for police raises "to arrest the alarming number of resignations from the department," in the hope that the state legislature would follow through with a special "deficiency appropriation" when it convened the following January. "If this 'extraordinary' gamble fails, the Mayor said, 'difficult and painful' cuts will have to be made in other city departments."

Other articles in May provided comparative information demonstrating the salary differential between Baltimore and other cities, and again noting the city's police strike in 1974 that led to the firing of "hundreds of officers" and the dismantling of the police union. After that, the *Sun* (5/6/79) reported, officers had no "voice in wage negotiations" and had "to accept whatever the city was willing to offer." When Governor Hughes at first failed to include the full "deficiency appropriation" in his budget proposal (*Sun*, 1/17/80), reporting focused on the riskiness of Mayor Schaefer's gamble in the first place. By early February, the governor had reversed his decision (*Sun*, 2/2/80), including in his proposal funds to cover Baltimore's deficit, but leaving Mayor Schaefer expressing caution at the prospects of future emergency appropriations from the state.

Affirmative Action in Police Hiring

With the police salary issue finally, although temporarily, resolved, a seven-year-old affirmative action suit brought against the city by an organization of black police officers (the Vanguard Justice Society) returned to the newspapers as federal court hearings continued in Baltimore. The headline, "Pomerleau Calls Women 'Balls of Fluff' In Bias Case" (*Sun*, 11/26/80) alluded to his comments three years earlier when he was a witness for the police department in one of the discrimination cases. The article indicated that a court ruling had been rendered in favor of the black male plaintiff's contention that the department's promotional tests were discriminatory. The court had also ruled that the department's height and weight requirements discriminated against women. The current case involved the allegation that the distribution of assignments and promotions worked to the disadvantage of women.

Baltimore in Retrospect

Baltimore reduced the size of its police force considerably (by over 350 officers) during the decade—to some extent as a result of the 1974 strike and the aftermath of "union busting," but also because of worries about the city's fiscal limitations and their impact on police funding. As in Detroit and Philadelphia, city officials did not cut other services to provide for policing.

The Baltimore Police Department was also under some affirmative action pressure. Testing practices were being revamped to comply with the expectation that they would not be biased against blacks; other police policy requirements and practices were under scrutiny by the courts to determine their fairness toward women.

Baltimore, like other old northeastern cities, had declined in population size and increased in poverty over the decade. With its new black majority, the city had scaled back the size of its police force after breaking its union. While Baltimore is unique as a case study, it joined Philadelphia and Detroit as a third example of the 1970s' decline in the acknowledged importance of the police in majority black cities.

Chicago

The Context

Chicago followed the 1970s' pattern of large cities outside the Sunbelt, declining in population size by about 360,000 and in population density from 15,000 per square mile to 13,000 (See Table 5.10). The incidence of poverty in the population increased from 11 percent to 17 percent from 1970 to 1980; blacks and Hispanics assumed a larger share of the city population, each 7 percent greater in 1980 than in 1970. Despite the increasing percentage of blacks and Hispanics in Chicago during the decade, there was no improvement in their economic situation; blacks, on average, earned only about 53 percent of what whites earned in 1980, in contrast to 71 percent in 1970. The increase in the crime rate from 38 to 65 crimes per thousand, while expected, did not keep up with the national growth in crime, taking Chicago from a point just above the average for large cities to a position considerably below the 1980 average of 81 crimes per thousand. The city's reported police expenditures for salaries, operations, and capital items in 1978, at $113 per capita, were considerably above the $48 average figure for large cities, and were $59 per capita greater than predicted by our equation. Capital police expenditures alone were just below the predicted level.

Police Brutality: Its Legacy Eclipsed by Other Police Improprieties

Police-related newspaper reporting in Chicago in 1979 and 1980 reflected the legacy of the city's past. Continued allegations of police brutality toward blacks and Puerto Ricans were discussed (*Chicago Tribune*, 9/24/80; *Daily Defender*, 6/12/80, 9/24/80, 9/29/80), as was the investigation of the 1969 Black Panther shootout in which two Panther leaders were killed (*Chicago Tribune*, 4/24/79). However, more than in the past, reporting focused on other questionable

Table 5.10
Chicago Profile

Characteristic	1970	1980
Population Size	3367 thsnd	3005 thsnd
Population Density	15099 sqmi	13174 sqmi
Per Capita Revenue	$183	$587
Per Cent Poor	11%	17%
Per Cent Black	33%	40%
Per Cent Hispanic	7%	14%
Black/White Median Income	.71	.53
Crime Rate Per Thousand	38	65
Police Expenditures Per Capita		
Total	$62	$113
Salaries/Operations	$61	$112
Capital	$1.4	$1.1

practices of Chicago police officers such as (1) routine strip searches of women stopped for committing minor traffic violations while driving without a valid driver's license (*Chicago Sun-Times,* 2/14/79; *Washington Post,* 2/16/79); (2) a scandal involving theft of automobile parts and electronic materials (*Chicago Tribune,* 8/28/79, 8/29/79, 8/31/79); (3) a phony invoice scheme relating to the motor pool and electronics divisions (*Chicago Tribune,* 8/28/79, 8/31/79); (4) allegations of a "... Cop 'Gun Plot'" (*Chicago Sun-Times,* 9/29/80, 9/28/80) involving police provision of guns for use by the mob; and (5) a top level shake-up of police leadership amid charges of their fiscal inefficiency and loyalty to politics rather than to the community, leading to Mayor Byrne's initiation of a search for a new police superintendent (*Chicago Sun-Times,* 10/13/79, 8/11/79, 8/15/79, 8/16/79; *Chicago Tribune,* 4/21/79, 10/10/79, 10/13/79, 7/24/79, 8/16/79).

Police Layoffs: Fiscal Exigencies and Loss of
Public Confidence in the Police

Staffing issues also moved to the forefront of news reporting in Chicago at the end of the decade. Newspaper reports detailed the Teamsters' efforts to organize the police officers association; the reorganization of police patrol areas and implementation of one man squadrols as cost-cutting measures; and what the *Sun-Times* (10/22/79) alleged to be the understaffing of the police "to the thinnest point in a decade to save cash for Mayor Byrne's first budget." According to the *Sun-Times,* Mayor Byrne's quiet enforcement of "a police hiring freeze since she took office April 16" had led to the police department's being 750 officers short of its authorized strength of 13,203 by October 1, a deficit predicted to increase through normal attrition to 875 by the end of 1979.

While tense police/minority relations had certainly not left the city by 1979, attention to the issue was eclipsed by allegations of fiscal improprieties, mob/police connections, and by Mayor Byrne's reorganization of top police staff. The mayor's selection of a white candidate, Richard J. Brzeczek, as police superintendent over the two blacks on the three-person list submitted to her by the police board, led the Reverend Jesse Jackson to brand the pick "an extension of Mayor Byrne's racist policies" (*Chicago Tribune*, 1/12/80).

Chicago in Retrospect

The major difference between early- and late-in-the-decade police-related reporting in Chicago is the shift in its focus from intensive attention to police brutality toward minorities toward greater discussion of police improprieties, scandals, and allegations of the misuse of funds. In that context the announcement of the reductions in police force size that resulted from Mayor Byrne's hiring freeze came as no surprise. Public confidence in the effectiveness of the Chicago Police Department and in its use of funds had been shaken.

Newark

The Context

Changes in Newark's socioeconomic situation during the decade were largely predictable in light of national urban trends. By 1980, the city was slightly reduced in population size and density, like most other large urban centers outside the Sunbelt. The level of poverty had increased to 30 percent of the population; the ratio of black to white median income had slipped during the decade to a point where blacks earned, on average, 64 percent of what whites earned (see Table 5.11). This was down from 75 percent in 1970, and somewhat surprising as the proportion of whites in the city had decreased over the decade. By 1980 Hispanics constituted 19 percent of the population and blacks were 58 percent. City revenues overall, however, remained on the high side for cities of 50,000 or more, as did the city's crime rate at 129 crimes per thousand. The average for the large city subpopulation was 81 crimes per thousand.

Reported police expenditures in the city were quite high as well, about $100 per capita, in comparison to the $48 per capita average in the large city group, and about $16 greater than predicted by the city's crime rate, population size, population composition, and economic conditions. Expenditures for capital police items, however, were still less than expected. At $1.30 per capita they were $1 per capita less than the average for cities of 50,000 or more, and about $1.50 less than predicted by city characteristics. While fear of crime in the city may have been justifiably high, it may not have generalized into a desire to arm or otherwise equip the city's police officers.

Table 5.11
Newark Profile

Characteristic	1970	1980
Population Size	382thsnd	329 thsnd
Population Density	15917 sqmi	13662 sqmi
Per Capita Revenue	$425	$1237
Per Cent Poor	18%	30%
Per Cent Black	54%	58%
Per Cent Hispanic	7%	19%
Black/White Median Income	.75	.64
Crime Rate Per Thousand	83	129
Police Expenditures Per Capita		
Total	$64	$100
Salaries/Operations	$63	$99
Capital	$1.2	$1.3

Police Layoffs: Recognition That Programs,
not Police, Reduce Crime

By 1979, police-related headlines in Newark announced (1) the layoffs of 200 Newark officers and efforts to rehire them (*Star-Ledger,* 1/10/79, 1/22/79, 3/5/80); (2) continued police demands for a salary increase and threats of a police strike (*Star-Ledger,* 1/17/80, 1/22/80, 3/5/80); and (3) implementation of a program whereby Newark police would investigate only those crimes believed to be solvable (*Star-Ledger,* 2/1/79). Despite the city's extremely high crime rate, and despite the police officer's union's strenuous efforts to force their reinstatement, Newark was not a city willing to continue the high investment in police spending that had been characteristic of its past (*Star-Ledger,* 3/5/80).

Mayor Gibson's willingness to reduce the size of the police force, and his view that police force size had little to do with the crime rate, reflected the views of blacks in high crime areas. While blacks expressed high fear of crime, they rated other service provision areas in greater need of funding (cf. Heinz et al., 1979: 59, 79; *Star-Ledger,* 3/5/80). In 1978, several months before our review of the city's police-related news reporting, an article in the *Star-Ledger* summarized some of the Mayor's recent comments indicating that

the public has been sold a "bill of goods" that the more police a city has, the lower the crime rate. [In the mayor's words] The number of murders in high-crime areas would not change a fraction of a percent even if there were 15 patrolmen per block (Heinz et al., 1983: 87).

In 1980 (*Star-Ledger*, 3/5/80) "Gibson reiterated his contention that increased police manpower will not eliminate crime and called for additional community efforts. 'Citizens can be vigilant without being vigilantes,' he said." According to the *Star-Ledger*, Gibson said that it is unrealistic for citizens to expect police " 'to do the whole job of public safety by themselves. We must demand respect for ourselves, for the young and for the elderly.' . . . citizens must join the fight against 'crime annoyance.' "

Newark in Retrospect

A struggle for dominance was not being waged in Newark during the 1970s. Newark belonged to blacks by the end of the 1960s; with the election of Mayor Gibson in 1970, blacks governed the city as well. One legacy of the white era of the past was a large police force that was gradually diminished during the 1970s. Capital police expenditures in the city, however, never suggested the buildup of a weapons arsenal in the manner characteristic of some cities where blacks and whites were engaged in a struggle for dominance.

By 1980 police layoffs had reduced the size of the force by so many that the city council overrode (by 6 to 2) Mayor Gibson's veto of a measure to establish a police minimum (*Star-Ledger*, 10/24/80). The vote was in response to demands by several community organizations for more police protection. Mayor Gibson defended his veto and continued resistance to the measure on the grounds of its possible negative impact on other city departments deemed more important.

IMPLICATIONS

The results in this chapter provide evidence of the influence of social context on the relationship between minority group threat and the collective response to crime. Chapter 3 described the impact of the relative size of the black population on municipal fiscal commitment to policing in the early 1970s when the federal government viewed blacks as the major threat to national stability. The relationship between percent black and capital police spending was represented by the threat curve described by Blalock (1967) as escalating in terms of the mobilization of police resources but dropping off where blacks were a majority of the population. This chapter considered the cities later in the decade when, as national concerns about blacks subsided and attention turned to "emerging ethnic groups" (including those designated by the Census Bureau as "Hispanic"), the impact of Hispanic visibility on public commitment to crime control increased in importance. While the threat curve no longer depicted the percent black/capital expenditures relationship in 1978, it was characteristic of the Hispanic/salaries and operations relationship nationally and in the southern and western subpopulation of cities. End-of-the-decade reductions in federal funding for municipal police spending on capital items, a consequence of the view that anti-riot mobilization was no longer perceived to be necessary, may also have been reflected in the lack of significant impact of minority size on municipal capital police appropriations in 1978.

Another important comparison between the early and late 1970s' relationship of minority group threat to social control resource determination was the impact of the ratio of black to white median income. As the individual city profiles illustrate, many U.S. cities witnessed noticeable declines in the ratio of black to white median income during the 1970s. [Wilson's (1987) recent work explains and illustrates the reasons for these declines.] At the same time, the decade also witnessed an increased impact of the ratio of black to white median income on public support for social control. Early in the decade this measure of inequality was not a significant predictor of any category of police expenditures nationally or in the large and small city subpopulations. By 1978 it was a consistent predictor of capital police expenditures nationally and in the large city subpopulation, suggesting that the generalized black threat characteristic of the early part of the decade had become more clearly defined in terms of economic competition. After taking account of the effect of city revenues and poverty, cities in which blacks' income approached that of whites spent more on capital policing items.

For the large industrial cities discussed in this chapter, the decade was a time in which the salience of race and the importance of police brutality continued, but it was also a period of gradual movement away from municipal reliance on the police and on the law-and-order approach to the reduction of crime. As blacks grew in relative population size in these cities, achieving or approaching numerical majority, citizen demands for police accountability and fiscal cutbacks constrained the municipal police agenda. Citizens assumed greater control over police policy making. Curbs were placed on police use of deadly force and new codes of ethics specified severe sanctions for excessive use of force by police officers. Police layoffs and reductions in the police budget also signaled declines in public faith in the ability and power of the police to fight crime.

Blacks, who were most likely to be adversely affected by crime, were also most likely to be skeptical of police ability to control crime. By the end of the decade in Detroit, a majority black city, a civilian board of police commissioners set police policy, and U.S. Representative John Conyers (from Detroit) called for an emphasis on programs to combat social problems rather than more police officers to combat crime. In Philadelphia, every police officer was expected to be a public relations officer, and cutbacks in the size of the force were accompanied by newspaper articles citing the demographic determinants of crime as supporting a positive criminogenic forecast for the city during the next decade. In Baltimore, the police union was crippled, and the size of the force severely cut back. A hiring freeze reduced the size of the force in Chicago, after lengthy and intense investigation of police misuse of funds and other allegations of police impropriety. In Newark, Mayor Gibson reduced the city's investment in policing in favor of other city services, making clear his view that increasing the size of the police force would have no effect on the crime rate. In the next chapter we turn our attention to mid-sized cities where the relative size of the minority populations increased but did not approach numerical majority by the end of the decade.

6

Mid-Sized Cities at the
End of the Decade

Four of the mid-sized cities considered in Chapter 4 began the decade at the low
end of the spending continuum, and remained under or at expected levels in
1978. Minneapolis, Wichita, Sacramento, and Tulsa bucked the national trend
early in the decade—their levels of capital police spending were lower than
average (and lower than expected on the basis of their social and economic
characteristics) even when federal funding was available and in vogue. We will
next ask why, and try to assess the changes during the 1970s in cities that were
out of the national urban mainstream of police spending early in the decade.

In some of these cities, like Tulsa and Wichita, low police spending early in
the decade may have been a reflection of a general lack of focus on policing
among city residents as there was a dearth of news reporting on the subject.
While the focus of news reporting changed during the decade in Wichita, with
issues of race and policing increasing in salience in the 1970s, police
expenditures of all types remained on the low side in 1978.

Police spending in Minneapolis, in contrast, exhibited a relative increase
during the decade. News reporting reflected an undercurrent of concern at the
end of the decade about police brutality, but political intrusions in policing, and
corruption on the force were the foci of reporting. In Sacramento, recognition of
cultural diversity and greater representation on the force appeared to be the
decade's watchwords for police officials.

The relative size of the minority population in each of these cities was small,
with the combined population for blacks and Hispanics exceeding 14 percent
only in Sacramento, where just over one-quarter of the city population was
minority, evenly divided between Hispanics and blacks. The small size, and
hence the relative invisibility of the minority population in these cities, may have
had much to do with their relatively low levels of police spending per capita and

the overall lack of public concern about issues of hostility between police and community. This relationship will be in the forefront of our discussion as we investigate the individual cities in this group.

Minneapolis

The Context

By 1980 Minneapolis was a smaller city (by about 60,000 residents) than it had been in 1970 (see Table 6.1). While there was little growth in the relative size of the city's Hispanic population, the proportion black had doubled to close to 8 percent, and blacks were worse off vis-à-vis whites, as indicated by the decline in the ratio of black to white median income from 0.73 to 0.61. The percentage poor grew only slightly to 9 percent, while revenues per capita rose from the 1970 mean of $195 to $696, a point considerably above the mean for 1980.

The crime rate, 97 per thousand, was also higher than the large city average of 81 crimes per thousand. Police expenditures rose during the decade from their close to average position in 1971 to $65 per capita, noticeably above the 1978 average and about $10 per capita more than expected on the basis of the city's sociodemographic characteristics. This greater than expected spending was concentrated in salaries and operations where overall spending was about $12 greater than expected. Spending for capital items and facilities, at less than 15 cents per capita, was $1.70 per capita under expected spending levels.

Table 6.1
Minneapolis Profile

Characteristic	1970	1980
Population Size	434 thsnd	371 thsnd
Population Density	7884 sqmi	6732 sqmi
Per Capita Revenue	$195	$696
Per Cent Poor	7%	9%
Per Cent Black	4%	8%
Per Cent Hispanic	.9%	1.3%
Black/White Median Income	.73	.61
Crime Rate Per Thousand	54	97
Police Expenditures Per Capita		
Total	$26	$65
Salaries/Operations	$26	$65
Capital	$.2	$.1

Political Influences: Police Corruption

End-of-the-decade newspaper reporting in Minneapolis focused on the extent to which city politics influenced the police force (*Minneapolis Tribune, 7/23/79, 11/1/80*), the link between prostitution and police corruption in the city (*Minneapolis Tribune, 7/29/79a,b, 7/31/79a,b*), financial problems of the police pension fund (*Minneapolis Tribune, 6/12/79*), and a plan to train more minority police (*Minneapolis Tribune, 6/20/79*).

July and August police-related articles quoted the insider's view that "you don't rise on merit, but on political connections" (*Minneapolis Tribune, 7/29/79a*), and headlined ". . . Political Influences Ruining Police Force" (*Minneapolis Tribune, 8/4/79a*). In August Deputy Police Chief James O'Meara charged that the Minneapolis Police Department was "being ruined by 'pervasive political influences,'" calling his association with its administration "a personal and professional embarassment" (*Minneapolis Tribune, 8/4/79a*).

Program to Train Minority Police

Amid these allegations, a plan to train minority police was announced (*Minneapolis Tribune, 6/20/79*). Financed by the federal Comprehensive Education and Training Act (CETA), the program was established to train the unemployed and underemployed. The Minneapolis two-year plan, to cost $700,000, would train 50 poor and minority people to become Minneapolis police officers.

The 1979 report in the *Tribune* (6/20/79) indicated that of 754 sworn officers in Minneapolis at the time, 9 were black males, 6 were American Indian males, and 7 were white females. One Chicano male and one black female were also among the ranks. Referring to the recruiting plan, Mr. Dziedzic, the alderman of the first ward [also reported to be a police officer (*Tribune, 11/1/80*)] said that the plan " 'is the only way I know to solve some of the problems facing the city in police minority relationships.' If minority officers work along with white officers . . . 'it'll do away with more than half of the citizen complaints we get.' Many complaints against the police now charge racial prejudice, he said" (*Minneapolis Tribune, 6/20/79*).

The program, its prospects, and the issue of police/community relations did not receive extensive coverage, however. Police-related newspaper reporting in the city centered for the next few months on the problem of political intrusions into the work of the police department (*Minneapolis Tribune, 7/23/79, 7/29/79b, 7/31/79a, 8/4/79a,b, 8/7/79, 8/10/79, 8/19/79, 9/5/79*).

Police Chief's Resignation

By August 7, the editor of the Minneapolis Police Officers Federation newsletter asked for the resignation of Police Chief Elmer Nordlund in the wake of a scandal in the vice squad and allegations that Nordlund "had covered up at least two instances of alleged impropriety by members of the Vice Squad"

(*Minneapolis Tribune,* 8/7/79). David Niebur, author of the newsletter, stated that "Elmer Nordlund can't be blamed for all the politics in the department. He can only be blamed for perpetuating it. . . . He is a product of those politics that have permeated this department for almost a hundred years." Since January Minneapolis newspapers had tied corruption to the link between politics and police appointments, indicating as Niebur did in August (*Minneapolis Tribune,* 8/7/79), that "policemen who work for a successful mayoral candidate get good jobs after the election." The police chief himself concurred in this assessment, indicating that "the only way to get the politics out of the department is to pick a strong police chief from outside of it" and to give the chief a three-year term of office, rather than continuing the existing pattern by which he serves at the pleasure of the mayor (*Minneapolis Tribune,* 8/7/79).

Chief Nordlund resigned shortly after these allegations, and was succeeded by Don Dwyer, amid lame duck Mayor Hofstede's public expressions of trust in Nordlund (*Minneapolis Tribune,* 8/10/79). Dwyer's term was set to last four and one-half months, until a new mayor took office. Dwyer was the ninth Minneapolis police chief in eleven years. Soon after Nordlund's resignation, serious discussion of the need for establishment of a three-year term of office began, a procedure that would require a change in the city charter (*Minneapolis Tribune,* 8/26/79).

In September, as the scandal over vice squad improprieties settled down, news reporting focused on the Internal Affairs Unit of the police department. Before an advisory committee of the U.S. Commission on Civil Rights, the Internal Affairs Unit was faulted on four counts: (1) propriety of complaint investigation; (2) disciplining of officers and speed of their criminal prosecution; (3) revision of department policies "to prevent future abuses"; (4) compensation of victims of police abuse. In making the allegations, Hennepin County Attorney Tom Johnson argued that the city ought to hire someone from outside the force to review complaints of police misconduct (*Minneapolis Tribune,* 9/28/79).

Police/Community Relations: An Improvement

The post-election (mayoral) reporting of 1980 reflected a better public image of the police department. In late July an article in the *Minneapolis Tribune* (7/25/80) announced in its headline, "Police Brutality Complaints Fall By Half In Minneapolis This Year," and reported 11 complaints of mishandling by the police for the first half of 1980. The fact that "the department has been run by two men who are considered strong disciplinarians" since August 1979, was cited as important to the turnaround.

In October, Bruce Lindberg, a 30-year police force veteran known for his work in community affairs, accepted appointment as head of the police Internal Affairs Unit. This appointment was welcomed by the executive director of the city's Urban League, who noted, though, that "many minority members have complained about the police department through the internal affairs unit . . . [and in] . . . 'many cases don't think they've gotten satisfactory results.'" Lindberg indicated his hope for change in the system, preferably the development of a unit outside of the force, responsible for judging complaints against the police (*Minneapolis Tribune,* 10/17/80).

Finally, in response to police reorganization efforts moving some officers from low- to high-crime precincts, there was a city council effort to establish a police officer minimum of 50 in each precinct. But political jockeying among the ward representatives prevented more than a 7-6 vote in its favor, and Police Chief Bouza indicated that he would not honor the resolution in dispersing his officers (*Minneapolis Tribune,* 11/1/80).

Minneapolis Retrospective

Throughout the decade of the 1970s, the combined percentage of blacks and Hispanics in Minneapolis remained under 10 percent, although the relative size of the black population increased from 4 percent to 8 percent. Both expenditures for capital police items and newspaper reporting suggest that blacks were not a major threat to the residents or police of the city. However, the doubling of the relative size of the black population during the decade may have exacerbated the problems of brutality, alluded to in police-related news reporting of 1979 and 1980, but not dealt with directly. The need for more recruiting of minority officers and problems of police/minority relationships were alluded to but not discussed clearly or extensively. While they were an undercurrent to end-of-the-decade reporting on vice squad improprieties and the problem of political influence in police appointment procedures and operations, they were not scrutinized by the press. It may be that the intensity of public dissatisfaction with political intrusions in police hiring and corruption on the force did not leave room for press concern with police/minority relations. Or it may be that although the problem was beginning to emerge, its resolution was not high on the public agenda.

Despite the fact that capital expenditures were lower than expected in Minneapolis, expenditures for police salaries and operations were higher than expected in 1978. This may have been the result of the political patronage and corruption described in city news accounts. Law and order issues did not appear to be high on the public agenda in Minneapolis.

Tulsa

The Context

Tulsa's population increased by about 30,000 between 1970 and 1980; the black proportion grew to about 12 percent (see Table 6.2). Some improvement in the city's economic climate was reflected in (1) the rise of the ratio of black to white median income from 49 percent to 57 percent over the ten year period; (2) the reduction in percent poor from 9 percent to 7.4 percent; and (3) the increase

Table 6.2
Tulsa Profile

Characteristic	1970	1980
Population Size	330 thsnd	361 thsnd
Population Density	1922 sqmi	1945 sqmi
Per Capita Revenue	$111	$541
Per Cent Poor˙	9%	7%
Per Cent Black	10%	12%
Per Cent Hispanic	1.4%	1.7%
Black/White Median Income	.49	.57
Crime Rate Per Thousand	38	89
Police Expenditures Per Capita		
Total	$14	$39
Salaries/Operations	$14	$38
Capital	$.26	$1.4

in per capita revenues from $111 per capita, a level considerably below the 1970 average for southern cities of 50,000 or more, to $541 per capita, a level closer to the 1978 regional average of $573 per capita. Tulsa's 1980 crime rate, at 89 crimes per thousand, just about matched the national average; but police expenditures in 1978 remained below average at $39 per capita overall (about $5 per capita less than expected given the city's crime rate, revenues, and other characteristics), and at $1.40 per capita for capital expenditures (less than expected by about 50 cents per capita).

Consistent with the generally low level of expenditures for police protection in Tulsa is the low level of newspaper coverage of issues relating to police/community interaction or police recruitment of minorities at the end of the decade. These were minimally reported issues in Tulsa in 1972, and there is no indication that their coverage increased significantly by the end of the decade.

Tulsa in Retrospect

Tulsa, a moderately large southern city with a small, but visible black population, allocated less funding for policing than expected early in the decade, but publicly discussed the need for minority representation on the police force in the midst of extensive investigation into an incident of alleged police brutality. At the end of the decade policing was still not high on the city agenda, with the level of expenditures remaining on the low side, and little mention of police/community relations issues in city newspapers.

Wichita

The Context

Wichita's population did not change appreciably between 1970 and 1980, increasing only slightly to 279,000 (see Table 6.3). The relative size of the city's poor, black, and Hispanic populations also remained relatively stable at 11 percent and 3 percent respectively. Economically, however, the city's blacks did not fare as well vis-à-vis whites as they once had; in 1980 they earned an average of 59 percent of whites' median income, as opposed to the 62 percent they earned in 1970. The crime rate more than doubled over the course of the decade, but did not deviate sharply from the average for cities of 50,000 or more. Police expenditures also doubled, but at $35 per capita, remained (by about $12 per capita) below the level expected on the basis of the city's sociodemographic characteristics. Both salaries/operations and capital police spending were lower than predicted (by about $11 and $1.30 per capita respectively). Revenues per capita, however, increased considerably from $159, a point below the 1970 mean of $195, to $656 per capita, a point considerably above the 1980 large city mean of $559.

Police Brutality

Reporting in early 1979 focused on the issue of police brutality, stemming initially from an incident in December 1978, in which three black youths, who admitted to embezzing $5 worth of gasoline from a convenience store, were allegedly shot at, subjected to racial slurs, and beaten by police officers after a

Table 6.3
Wichita Profile

Characteristic	1970	1980
Population Size	277 thsnd	279 thsnd
Population Density	3197 sqmi	2754 sqmi
Per Capita Revenue	$159	$656
Per Cent Poor	8%	7%
Per Cent Black	10%	11%
Per Cent Hispanic	2%	3%
Black/White Median Income	.62	.59
Crime Rate Per Thousand	40	88
Police Expenditures Per Capita		
Total	$16	$35
Salaries/Operations	$16	$35
Capital	$.3	$.5

high speed chase (*Wichita Eagle*, 1/6/79, 1/18/79a, 1/18/79b, 1/19/79, 2/23/79). In the midst of demands for a federal probe of the incident, a previously planned federal civil rights hearing began in the city as part "of a nationwide investigation of relations between communities and their law enforcement agencies" (*Wichita Eagle*, 2/17/79).

At the hearing "State Senator Bill McCray and Wichita State University Professor Bernice Hutcherson, both black Wichitans, told the committee there are genuine feelings of mistrust and fear pervading the black community" (*Wichita Eagle*, 2/17/79). Police Chief LaMunyon largely dismissed these allegations, noting that while the situation wasn't perfect, the department was working toward improved police/community relations.

In April an incident that the press termed a riot was sparked by a confrontation between police and the crowd of 3500 at a Herman Hill rock concert (*Wichita Eagle*, 4/17/79, 4/19/79). Police were charged with brutality and excessive use of force. Forty people were injured, 28 of them officers. Altogether 88 people were arrested during the incident.

Later in the year the *Wichita Eagle* (6/24/79) investigated the extent of the problem of police brutality, looking into the "way in which the Wichita Police Department and the Sedgwick County Sheriff's Office do that job." The article noted that during the past three years, "scores of highly publicized charges of police brutality have been brought forth." The paper presented a list of charges and countercharges, noting the emotionalism on both sides (*Wichita Eagle*, 6/24/79, 6/28/79).

Subsequent articles were headlined, "Black Perspective: A Picture of Distrust, Fear, and Resentment" (*Wichita Eagle*, 6/25/79), outlining the tension within the black community between the desire for more law enforcement—of a high quality—and the desire of some blacks to keep police out of black communities; and "Police: Duty Calls, But So Does Reality" (*Wichita Eagle*, 6/27/79), discussing the split in police officers' perspectives, between those who were aware of "officers who shouldn't be wearing badges," given their racist attitudes and persistent use of physical force, and those officers who were baffled by the frequent charges of brutality. The constant stress police officers face and their alienation from the black communities they serve were cited as elements that turn people with good intentions into sometimes abusing officers.

Civilian Review Board

In March, discussion of proposals to create a civilian review board to investigate complaints against the police received some consideration in the press (*Wichita Eagle*, 3/27/79). Police Chief Richard LaMunyon and all six candidates for City Commission were opposed to the idea (*Wichita Eagle*, 5/18/79).

Police Use of Deadly Force

The Kansas Advisory Committee to the U.S. Civil Rights Commission described in August a "'profound disparity in the perception of police activity' by citizens and public servants," with many witnesses indicating that police/community relations "have been strained to the breaking point" and that deadly force is used too liberally by the city's officers. In fact, the report suggested that the Kansas statute "regulating the use of deadly force is too broad compared with other states' statutes and federal guidelines suggested by national organizations" (*Wichita Eagle*, 8/14/79).

October reporting (*Wichita Eagle*, 10/12/79) indicates that the Wichita branch of the NAACP filed a complaint in U.S. District Court alleging that police department practices in the city were racially discriminatory and violated provisions in the U.S. Constitution. Improper uses of deadly force and other alleged abusive actions were listed in the complaint.

Police-related reporting in 1980 began with an article entitled "Police Limit Arms Use," describing the new, "more restrictive policy on shooting at suspects" (*Wichita Eagle*, 1/15/80). The new policy "limits the situations in which officers can fire at suspects and forbids certain types of weapons and ammunition . . . by on- and off-duty officers."

Police Force: Discrimination in Hiring and Promotions

In addition to brutality, affirmative action in hiring was a big end-of-the-decade issue in Wichita. Prentice Lewis, associate director of the Urban League, charged that "The city of Wichita . . . is not an equal opportunity employer." Robert L. Palacioz, job developer for the Hispanic employment group SER, claimed that minorities were seriously discouraged from applying for police positions due to tokenism, low advancement opportunity, and ostracism by colleagues and neighbors (*Wichita Eagle*, 2/16/79).

Wichita in Retrospect

Clearly, by the end of the decade, Wichitans' attention was focused, at least through their newspapers, on problems and issues of police/community relations (*Wichita Eagle*, 5/13/80). Neither the size of the minority population (11 percent black, 3 percent Hispanic) nor its growth during the decade (percent black and percent Hispanic each increased by 1 percent) led to the expectation that minority/police relations should have been so much more acrimonious at the end of the decade than they were at the beginning, but that is what the newspapers reflect.

After the city's two riots in the latter part of the 1960s, it is possible that 1972 was the aberrant period, with police unusually community-oriented, and the minority community unusually cooperative toward police. It may also be that the U.S. Civil Rights Commission's national investigation of relations between black communities and law enforcement organizations brought some of these problems to the fore and led the press to focus on them in 1979. In any case, Wichita's level of police spending in 1978 was still considerably below the level expected on the basis of the city's social and economic characteristics; it was also considerably below the average figures for large cities. While black Wichitans took the threat posed by their police seriously enough to make public their complaints about mistreatment and brutality, white Wichitans, clearly in the majority, had not yet been motivated to fortify their police as a source of protection.

Sacramento

The Context

Population in Sacramento grew by about 20,000 between 1970 and 1980; city revenues grew from $191 per capita to $499, remaining at about the national average (see Table 6.4). The city experienced very slight increases in the percentage poor, black, and Hispanic over the decade; the ratio of black to white median income remained unchanged at 0.67. Increase in the crime rate by 1980 to 126 per thousand reflected the increase in the national urban average, with the 1980 rate two and one-half times higher than it was a decade earlier. Expenditures for police salaries and operations grew to $64 per capita overall, about $14 greater than predicted on the basis of the city's social and economic characteristics. Capital expenditures, however, slipped to less than $.20 per capita, about $2.60 per capita less than expected.

Police-related news reporting in Sacramento in 1979 was limited to a brief on contract negotiations at the county level (*Sacramento Bee,* 2/2/79) and an article discussing the effectiveness of the probation patrol system (*Sacramento Bee,* 3/11/79). Reporting in 1980 included a piece about the swift police response time in the city of Sacramento (in comparison to the county) to life threatening calls, the need for more officers and updated, computerized dispatching equipment (*Sacramento Bee,* 12/22/80).

Mid-year an article (*Sacramento Bee,* 7/16/80) described a three-hour rally at City Hall by a Mexican-American group (the South Sacramento Watch Action Group) protesting alleged police harassment of "low-riders, usually Mexican-American youths who cruised in specially altered cars. . . ." The group asked the city council for a recreational center as an alternative for young people. "The Council also heard specific accounts of alleged police harassment by three low-riders, all of whom said they can't drive their cars down the street without being pulled over by police." The Sacramento Police Department argued that they issued three times as many traffic tickets at downtown Sacramento's loop frequented mostly by Caucasians.

Sacramento in Retrospect

Newspaper reporting and police expenditure review in Sacramento present a consistent picture of a city working to meet its black (13 percent) and Hispanic

Table 6.4
Sacramento Profile

Characteristic	1970	1980
Population Size	257 thsnd	276 thsnd
Population Density	2741 sqmi	2869 sqmi
Per Capita Revenue	$191	$499
Per Cent Poor	11%	12%
Per Cent Black	11%	13%
Per Cent Hispanic	13%	14%
Black/White Median Income	.67	.67
Crime Rate Per Thousand	46	126
Police Expenditures Per Capita		
Total	$36	$64
Salaries/Operations	$35	$64
Capital	$1	$.2

(14 percent) demands for greater representation on the force and more recognition of cultural diversity. Tension between the police and minority communities did not appear to have reached hostile levels. In addition, while the city spent more than expected on police salaries and operations, its outlays for capital items continued to be under expected levels.

SUMMARY AND IMPLICATIONS

The cities reviewed in this chapter illustrate changes initiated during the 1970s in municipal police priorities and in police/community relations. In Minneapolis early-in-the-decade race and ethnic relations were not reflected in city newspapers as a major police concern. After the relative size of Minneapolis' black population doubled, from 4 percent to 8 percent, end-of-the-decade reporting contained an undercurrent of concern about race relations, as citizen complaints of police officers' racial bias and efforts to recruit more minorities on the force were mentioned. These issues, however, were not major ones in the press. Capital police spending remained low throughout the decade, while problems of corruption and political influence on the police force assumed major importance. Problems of race relations were present in Minneapolis in 1978, but they were not the focus of police resource mobilization and policy.

Tulsa completed the decade as it had begun it, with a low level of police expenditures (for a city of its size) and little focus on problems of minority/police relations. In Wichita, blacks' complaints of police brutality and racial bias were evident in end-of-the-decade reporting. Police spending in all categories remained below average and below expected levels given city characteristics. The small size of Wichita's black (10%) and Hispanic (2.5%) populations in 1970 may have prevented whatever threat these groups posed from triggering increases in police resources in either the capital or salaries/operations areas.

Sacramento, like Minneapolis, evidenced little direct focus on police issues relating to race and ethnicity during the decade. Some complaints of police brutality, one of which had racial overtones, were reported in 1972; in 1980 allegations of police harassment of Mexican-American youths cruising in customized cars surfaced. A public hearing was held on this issue, but neither the issue nor related police items received much attention in the city's press.

Overall, at the end of the decade, these mid-sized cities with relatively small minority populations reflected the decline of capital police spending that was observed nationally although there was no noticeable withdrawal of their fiscal commitment to salaries and operations. Police layoffs did not figure prominently on the public agenda, as they had in the large industrial, majority (or close-to-majority) black cities; neither did the development of mechanisms for greater police accountability. Cities where blacks and Hispanics constituted a small, relatively invisible proportion of the population appeared to continue the traditional police/community agenda with somewhat more attention devoted to minority concerns by the end of the decade.

7

A Decade's Change in Southern and Western Cities

Regional context influences the level of threat engendered by racial and ethnic groups by filtering majority perceptions of specific minority groups. The evidence in Chapter 4 indicated that even after socioeconomic variations are controlled, the impact of minority size on public fiscal commitment to policing is greater in those regions where the minority group's history of interaction with whites has been characterized by greatest tension or conflict.

The continuing significance of racial/ethnic relations in social control resource determination, and its links to shifts in the federal focus from blacks to other minorities were illustrated in Chapter 5. Because the influence of percent Hispanic increased in importance nationally, but especially in cities of the South and West, and since the expenditures model retained over the decade much more of its explanatory power in the South than elsewhere, it appears that there is some stability in the link between region and the perceptions of minority threat.

This chapter updates to 1978 the five cities in the South and West discussed in Chapter 4, with special attention to the influence of region on the changes during the decade.

Albuquerque

The Context

In 1980, Albuquerque was much the same as it was in 1970, with some improvement in its economic situation. Like other cities in the Sunbelt, its population increased slightly, from 244,000 to 332,000, as did the overall level of prosperity. The proportion of city residents with incomes below the poverty level declined (from 11% in 1970 to 9%) and the ratio of black to white median income increased (from 66% to 69%) (see Table 7.1). The relative size of its Hispanic and black populations remained the same. The city's revenues also showed considerable improvement, increasing from an average position relative to other cities of the South and the West to a slightly above average position.

In the face of the city's improved economic situation, the crime rate increased only moderately. Reported expenditures for police salaries and operations in 1978 were on target for the time period and region, while capital expenditures were high—about twice the average and close to $2 per capita greater than predicted on the basis of Albuquerque's crime rate, economic, and other characteristics.

Newspaper reporting in Albuquerque in 1979 and 1980 provides little information relating to police/community relations or police funding issues. Anglo/Hispanic tension did not assume a prominent role in the police-related news reporting of the time. One 1979 article (*Albuquerque Journal*, 5/1/79) detailed charges by a fired police officer that his dismissal, ostensibly for conduct unbecoming an officer and other infractions, really resulted from biases relating to his Hispanic heritage and his pro-citizen stand on police brutality cases. Another article (*Albuquerque Journal*, 2/26/80) described fiscal shortfalls for an undercover sting operation program funded until 1979 by the Law Enforcement Assistance Administration. While capital spending remained high, public attention, at least in the press, did not focus on issues of minority representation or control of police operations.

Table 7.1
Albuquerque Profile

Characteristic	1970	1980
Population Size	244 thsnd	332 thsnd
Population Density	2965 sqmi	3481 sqmi
Per Capita Revenue	$154	$537
Per Cent Poor	11%	9%
Per Cent Black	2%	2%
Per Cent Hispanic	35%	34%
Black/White Median Income	.66	.69
Crime Rate Per Thousand	55	88
Police Expenditures Per Capita		
Total	$28	$45
Salaries/Operations	$22	$41
Capital	$6.5	$4

Albuquerque in Retrospect

In Albuquerque, a southwestern city with a large Hispanic population, social control resource allocation was high, early and late in the decade. News reporting, especially in the early 1970s, brought some instances of Hispanic/police hostility to light. This hostility may have fueled public willingness to continue the city's high level of police spending to the end of the decade.

Denver

The Context

Some changes in Denver's socioeconomic characteristics were evident by 1980. Overall, city population size dropped slightly, from 515,000 to 492,000; the proportion of blacks in the population increased to 12 percent and Hispanics to 19 percent (see Table 7.2). The ratio of black to white median income declined from 74 percent to 72 percent, and overall poverty increased by 1 percent to 10 percent. City revenues rose as well, remaining considerably above the average for cities in the region; as in 1970, the 1980 crime rate was higher at 119 per thousand than the region's urban average of 85 per thousand population.

Expenditures reported for all categories of policing were up sharply in 1978: $92 per capita overall, divided between $81 per capita for salaries and operations and $11 per capita for capital expenditures, both considerably above

Table 7.2
Denver Profile

Characteristic	1970	1980
Population Size	515 thsnd	492 thsnd
Population Density	4406 sqmi	4452 sqmi
Per Capita Revenue	$314	$875
Per Cent Poor	9%	10%
Per Cent Black	9%	12%
Per Cent Hispanic	17%	19%
Black/White Median Income	.74	.72
Crime Rate Per Thousand	74	119
Police Expenditures Per Capita		
Total	$29	$92
Salaries/Operations	$28	$81
Capital	$ 1	$11

the expected averages. Overall, 1970 police expenditures in Denver were $30 per capita greater than predicted on the basis of the city's crime rate and demographic and economic characteristics; expenditures for capital police items were about $8 per capita greater than expected.

Progress in Police/Community Relations

Newspaper accounts for 1979 and 1980 indicating Anglo/Hispanic or white/black tension are sparse. One related article in the *Rocky Mountain News* (2/19/79) may explain this. Entitled "Tensions Ease Between Police and Hispanos," the article described the reduction of violent confrontations and other hostile Anglo/Hispanic incidents. Citing comments by the president of the city council, himself a Chicano, the article indicated that while there were still instances of police abuse of Hispanics, the decade had witnessed considerable change in the social climate away from violent demonstrations toward greater police awareness of the environment in low income neighborhoods. The article also described improvements in the recruitment of Hispanics to the police force; by 1979, 170 of the city's 1400 officers were Hispanic, a considerable improvement from early in the decade.

Denver in Retrospect

Denver, like Albuquerque, was influenced by its southwestern location, but had a smaller Hispanic population and a larger black minority. Although Denver had low levels of police spending early in the decade, newspaper reporting indicated problems of minority representation on the police force, citing specific allegations of police brutality toward Hispanics, and to a lesser degree, toward blacks. As 1972 news reporting forewarned, and as could be expected on the basis of minority/police friction, by the end of the decade Denver's police spending had skyrocketed to levels greater than predicted on the basis of the city's crime rate, revenues, and other characteristics.

San Francisco

The Context

San Francisco experienced a population decline during the 1970s, losing about 35,000 residents (see Table 7.3). Its poverty rate and the relative size of its black population did not change appreciably, although the relative size of its Hispanic population decreased by 2 percent to 12 percent. Blacks were not as well off vis-à-vis whites at the end of the decade as they were at the beginning: The ratio of black to white median income declined from 0.69 to 0.62 from 1970 to 1980. The city's crime rate remained high, considerably above the average for cities of 50,000 or more, increasing to 104 crimes per thousand. Reported police expenditures overall increased to $85 per capita, with $2 per capita earmarked for capital items. Some reporting in 1979 described San Francisco's efforts to give all city workers, including police, "raises denied last year because of

Table 7.3
San Francisco Profile

Characteristic	1970	1980
Population Size	716 thsnd	679 thsnd
Population Density	15764 sqmi	14633 sqmi
Per Capita Revenue	$674	$1805
Per Cent Poor	10%	10%
Per Cent Black	13.4%	12.7%
Per Cent Hispanic	14%	12%
Black/White Median Income	.69	.62
Crime Rate Per Thousand	80	104
Police Expenditures Per Capita		
Total	$52	$85
Salaries/Operations	$51	$83
Capital	$1	$2

Proposition 13" (*San Francisco Examiner*, 5/3/79). Total expenditures were still under (by about $6 per capita) the level predicted on the basis of the city's demographic and economic characteristics. Capital expenditures were only about 30 cents per capita below the expected value, and were about 60 cents per capita lower than the average for large cities.

Police Force: Recruitment of Minority Officers

Police-related newspaper reporting in San Francisco in 1979 focused on the need, difficulties, and processes of minority recruitment, and on a proposed development of a police/community relations unit within the force. Stimuli for reporting in these areas included: (1) the out of court settlement of a six-year-old race and sex discrimination suit providing for recruitment of "at least 50 percent minorities and 20 percent women into the understaffed police force during the next ten years," and "payment by the City of $1.2 million to the plaintiffs, of which $500,000 would be used for recruitment, testing, and training" (*San Francisco Examiner*, 3/31/79; see also 2/28/79, 3/13/79, 7/7/79, 7/13/79, and *Sun Reporter*, 1/4/79, 3/1/79); (2) allegations of police brutality toward gays in the aftermath of the May 21 City Hall riot that erupted after the jury decision in the Dan White case rendered White guilty of voluntary manslaughter, not murder (*San Francisco Examiner*, 6/12/79, 6/16/79, 6/29/79).

The discrimination suit—brought in 1973 by public advocates on behalf of an organization of largely black police officers, Officers for Justice, and other minorities—alleged that minorities were underrepresented on the force, and discriminated against in employment opportunities. It eventually became a class action suit "for back pay and equal opportunity for entry and advancement" (*San Francisco Examiner,* 5/20/79).

As the *Examiner* (5/20/79) put it, "Everyone agreed . . . the courts, the United States government, all the minority officers involved in the class action suit [that the] police force, which was predominately white and male, in no way reflected the make up of San Francisco." The recruitment effort mandated by the settlement proved difficult, however, in the face of well-documented Latino and black suspicions toward the police, and the lack of female role models on the force. Chinese also needed to become accustomed to being wooed; they were "used to being discouraged from joining the force because they weren't tall enough" (*San Francisco Examiner,* 5/20/79). With new recruitment, San Francisco intended to fill 700 patrol jobs, greater than half the patrol force.

The recruitment drive ended in April, resulting in 7428 applications, including 1950 from white males, 733 from white females, 1244 from black males, 748 from black females, 803 from male Hispanics, 215 from female Hispanics, 557 from male Asians, 132 from female Asians, 401 from male Filipinos, and 84 from female Filipinos, 39 from American Indian males, 11 from American Indian females, 340 from undeclared males, and 168 from undeclared females (*San Francisco Examiner,* 5/20/79).

Post Dan White Verdict Violence: Brutality toward Gays

In May, the city was rocked by a violent disturbance—termed a riot in city newspapers—following the announcement of the jury decision finding former City Supervisor Dan White guilty of voluntary manslaughter—not murder—for the November 1978 killings of Mayor George Moscone and Supervisor Harvey Milk, a leader in the San Francisco gay community (*San Francisco Examiner,* 6/16/79).

According to a report by Police Chief Charles Gain for the Police Commission (*San Francisco Examiner,* 6/16/79), 129 police officers and 48 civilians were injured during the 6 hours of confrontations and $245,000 in damage to property occurred. Later reporting headlined, "Police Are Accused of Post-Riot Brutality" (*San Francisco Examiner,* 6/29/79); "City Hall Riot: Study Finds Cops Too Late and Too Few" (*San Francisco Examiner,* 11/1/79); "U.S. Investigating Police-Gay Incident" (*San Francisco Examiner,* 7/17/79).

Charges that too few officers responded to the scene too late, that San Francisco police did not have sufficient riot training, and that they were brutal toward gays led to continued discussion of (1) the need for more community relations training on the force (*San Francisco Examiner,* 7/13/79), and (2) significant efforts to attract more minorities to the force. The widespread belief that San Francisco police had failed in handling the riot situation (and in fact had brutalized gays in the post-riot aftermath) spurred the ouster of then Police Chief

Charles Gain (*Sun Reporter*, 6/21/79; *San Francisco Examiner*, 7/4/79, 7/6/79, 7/22/79). With a new chief, Cornelius Murphy, the San Francisco Police Commission continued into 1980 the reconsideration of development of a Police-Community Relations Division, scheduling open hearings to obtain minority input (*Sun Reporter*, 7/3/80, 7/17/80).

San Francisco in Retrospect

By the end of the 1970s questions of minority representation on the San Francisco police force and of police bias in confrontation control were not centered solely on black issues, or even on black and Hispanic complaints. Rather, they included efforts to recruit and meet with representatives of black, Hispanic, Asian, Filipino, American Indian, and female groups. The city's ethnic diversity was reflected in its recruitment targets. In addition, issues relating to the city's gays surfaced in newspaper reporting in reference to the recruitment drive. At community recruitment sessions, gays were quoted as having asked whether the process of self-identification of their sexual orientation would prevent them from being hired and make discrimination toward them by co-workers on the force inevitable.

The city's violent disturbance in 1978 involved gays—not blacks or Hispanics—and led to allegations of court bias and police brutality toward gays. San Francisco city officials seemed to be focusing on these police/community problems not through greater armament, but rather through efforts to obtain greater representation of these groups on the force, and through better training of police officers in handling confrontations.

Atlanta

The Context

By 1980, the city's population had decreased to about 425,000, with blacks then constituting 67 percent of the city's residents (see Table 7.4). The Hispanic population increased only slightly to 1.4 percent by 1980. Despite its location in the Sunbelt, Atlanta, like many northeastern and north central U.S. cities, during the 1970s experienced declining population and white flight, becoming increasingly a black community. However, like other cities of the Sunbelt, Atlanta was far more prosperous in 1980 than it had been a decade earlier. Its revenues in 1980, at $873 per capita, were almost double the mean revenue level for southern and western cities and noticeably higher than the $573 average for southern large cities, whereas it had not been far from the regional group mean in 1970. Despite the increase in per capita revenues, however, Atlanta's level of poverty, at 24 percent in 1980, was over twice that for southern and western cities overall, close to twice the figure for southern large cities, and noticeably greater than its own 16 percent figure of 1970. Similarly, the city's ratio of black to white median income declined during the decade from 61 percent to 48

Table 7.4
Atlanta Profile

Characteristic	1970	1980
Population Size	495 thsnd	425 thsnd
Population Density	3783 sqmi	3244 sqmi
Per Capita Revenue	$198	$873
Per Cent Poor	16%	24%
Per Cent Black	51%	67%
Per Cent Hispanic	1%	1.4%
Black/White Median Income	.61	.48
Crime Rate Per Thousand	55	140
Police Expenditures Per Capita		
Total	$32	$66
Salaries/Operations	$29	$64
Capital	$3.5	$2.5

percent, much lower than the regional large city average of 61 percent. Despite the white flight from the city reflected in the increasing proportion of blacks in the city population, inequality between blacks and whites increased in Atlanta during the 1970s, as did the overall poverty level of the urban population.

It is no surprise, then, that crime in Atlanta, at 140 crimes per thousand population in 1980, was over 50 percent greater than the rate for southern cities of 50,000 or more in population. Police expenditures in Atlanta had, by 1978, increased to $66 per capita, again higher than the regional large city average of $44 per capita, but still under (by about $1.60 per capita) the spending level predicted on the basis of the city's structural characteristics, revenues, and crime rate. Capital police expenditures in 1978, at $2.45 per capita, were in line with the $2 per capita average for southern large cities, but still under the expected value by about 58 cents per capita.

Tug of War for Control of the Police Bureaucracy

Considerable reporting at the end of the decade presents the details of what one article in the *Atlanta Journal* (3/29/79) referred to as "racial bickering and legal warfare between blacks and whites" with regard to the hiring and promotion of black officers and control of the city's police force (*Atlanta Journal*, 6/27/79, 11/13/79, 11/15/79). Mayor Maynard Jackson's proposal "to fill vacant ranking positions (72 in all) in the city police bureau with a 50-50 black-white quota system" was one element of the controversy (*Atlanta Journal*, 6/27/79). The president of Atlanta's predominantly white Fraternal Order of

Police objected and was quoted by the *Atlanta Journal* (6/27/79) as saying that "the city has been polarized long enough . . . ," while the president of the Afro-American Patrolmen's League hailed the plan as "a starting point. . . ." The article alluded to "a six-year-old court battle over racial criteria for hiring and promotions within the police department." Also under discussion was public consideration of proposals by a "large number of influential Atlanta lawyers and some Georgia politicians to shift control of the Atlanta police department from City Hall to the state Capital or to a consolidated county police authority" (*Atlanta Journal*, 11/11/79). The plans were being billed by proponents as a way to "remove the police department from local politics" (*Atlanta Journal*, 11/13/79). "But some key black leaders . . . [branded] the move as an attempt by the white establishment to dilute black political power by going outside the ballot box" (*Atlanta Journal*, 11/11/79; see also 11/15/79).

In addition to the issues of control of police policy and promotions, the low salary of Atlanta's police officers (*Atlanta Journal*, 1/18/79, 3/29/79, 4/11/79, 4/24/79, 11/12/79, 1/9/80, 1/25/80, 2/8/80), the general underfunding of policing in the city, the shortage of officers (*Atlanta Journal*, 1/18/79, 2/2/80, 4/10/79, 1/28/80, 3/30/80), and overcrowding in the police academy (*Atlanta Journal*, 11/10/80) were also issues at the end of the decade.

Atlanta in Retrospect

Atlanta, a majority black city that increased in proportion black throughout the decade, typified cities of that category with its generally low level of police spending persisting throughout the decade despite the city's overall affluence in terms of city revenues. By the end of the decade there was considerable police-related news reporting in the *Atlanta Journal,* but for the most part the reported racial tensions concerning policing focused heavily on issues of minority representation on, and control of the police force. Some incidents of racially directed brutality demonstrating police/community tension may have occurred, but they, and other types of police/minority hostility outside of the hiring issue, were not the subject of intensive newspaper reporting and investigation. This is as expected for majority black cities, where issues of dominance and control may no longer influence the public social control agenda, but where the last vestiges of white domination of the city political bureaucracy through entrenched civil service professionals and policies still remain.

Miami

The Context

By 1980, Miami's population, like that of other Sunbelt cities, had grown by 12,000 to 347,000. The relative proportion of blacks (25%) and Hispanics (56%) had increased as well; 20 percent of the city's population was poor, twice the national average (see Table 7.5). The ratio of black to white median income, at 0.63, was down from the 0.73 of 10 years earlier, indicating that blacks at the

Table 7.5
Miami Profile

Characteristic	1970	1980
Population Size	335 thsnd	347 thsnd
Population Density	9763 sqmi	10113 sqmi
Per Capita Revenue	$147	$473
Per Cent Poor	16%	20%
Per Cent Black	23%	25%
Per Cent Hispanic	45%	56%
Black/White Median Income	.73	.63
Crime Rate Per Thousand	71	151
Police Expenditures Per Capita		
Total	$32	$61
Salaries/Operations	$30	$60
Capital	$1.4	$.4

end of the decade were not as well off economically in comparison to whites as they had been in 1970. The city's crime rate, at 151 crimes per thousand, was almost twice the national average. City revenues, at $473 per capita, were still below the national average for large cities ($551 per capita), and below the regional large city mean ($573 per capita). Police expenditures overall also continued to be under expected levels (by about $7 per capita) even as predicted on the basis of the city's fiscal, demographic and other characteristics. Capital expenditures, at $.40 per capita, were about $2.40 per capita under the predicted level. Both deviations from predicted levels were much greater than they were in 1971, so it is unlikely that they were solely a consequence of the notorious overlaps in Miami's governmental structure.

Police Brutality: Continuing Problems

In 1979 Miami was still dealing with the same problems discussed in newspaper reporting earlier in the decade. An article in the *Miami Herald* (4/18/79), headlined "NAACP asks Federal Probe of Alleged Police Brutalities," described the NAACP's request to the U.S. Justice Department's civil rights division "to investigate brutality complaints involving Dade police forces . . . ." Later in the year, another article, "Agencies Seek Ways to Police the Police" (*Miami Herald,* 7/26/79a) indicated that Miami City Manager Joseph Grassie had a committee at work on police-review procedures. Miami Mayor Maurice Ferre announced that he was against both the extreme of "police judging themselves" and the extreme of "police not in the situation."

Articles throughout the summer of 1979 investigated police brutality, listing the names and records of the "two dozen Miami and Metro policemen repeatedly named in complaints of brutality" over the previous four years. For example, one article, entitled "Brutal Policemen Keep Badges, Guns" (*Miami Herald,* 7/22/79), pointed out that "those 24 policemen comprise about one per cent of the combined Metro and Miami force. Yet they are responsible for nearly a fifth of the 199 claims for money damages in brutality cases in the last four years. Most policemen generate few if any such claims."

The article also indicated that complaints against Miami police officers "increased 9.5 per cent in 1978"; that Miami had fired four officers for brutality in the past four years; that most "citizens who filed brutality complaints had not been arrested before the encounter in which they were injured"; that "most confrontations escalated from routine traffic stops or pedestrian encounters"; and that although "most brutality claimants are white . . . blacks . . . about a fifth of the local population file a . . . third of the brutality claims."

Another piece in the *Miami Herald* (7/23/79) offered "Metro's Meanest? A Look At 9 Officers," detailing each officer's history of brutality. In an article focused on city, not county police, the *Herald* (7/24/79) headlined "15 Officers Expensive For City," and described the claims against officers repeatedly accused of brutality.

Other related articles, entitled "Police Operate in World of Hostility" (*Miami Herald,* 7/25/79a) and "Stress of Job Makes Some Turn to Brutality" (*Miami Herald,* 7/25/79b), focused on the violence producing conditions of the police officer's job. An article on "Police Discipline Hidden in Secrecy" (*Miami Herald,* 7/26/79b) also discussed the problem of brutality in terms of public accountability.

The *Herald* sued to open the secret records of internal brutality investigations at both the Miami and Metro police departments. The paper explained that it listed "more repeaters in the Miami department because city police officials keep better records of brutality complaints and are more willing to release them, not because police are worse in Miami than at Metro." In fact, the *Miami Herald* (7/24/79) found that "most policemen generate few if any brutality claims."

The Miami Riot

Two celebrated 1979 allegations of police brutality in Dade County, both involving county (Metro), not Miami police officers, dominated 1980 police-related newspaper reporting in Miami. One incident involved the death of a black insurance executive during police apprehension; the other case involved a black schoolteacher allegedly beaten by Metro police after refusing to admit them to his home to serve a narcotics arrest warrant during a drug raid on the wrong house (*Miami Herald,* 2/27/79, 7/22/79, 1/4/80, 5/20/80, 12/22/80, 12/28/80, 12/30/80; *St. Petersburg Times,* 12/22/80; *Tallahassee Democrat,*

5/21/80). The *Miami Herald* (7/31/80, 8/6/80) investigated the backgrounds of the officers involved in both incidents, finding that all had multiple previous complaints filed against them.

The acquittal (by an all-white jury) of five white officers charged with manslaughter in the death of Arthur McDuffie, the black insurance executive, on May 17, 1980, precipitated a three-day riot in Liberty City and two other Miami neighborhoods. [See Porter and Dunn (1984) for a detailed account of the McDuffie incident, the alleged cover-up, court proceedings, and the riot.] In the aftermath of the riot, state and federal attention were focused on police brutality in Miami. [Although four Miami Police Department officers responded to the call for assistance, they were not involved in McDuffie's apprehension. The officers charged with manslaughter were all from the county (Metro) force.] On June 16, 1980, the *Herald* reported that "In an atmosphere of near-total secrecy, Miami federal grand juries this week will hear critical testimony as part of the U.S. Department of Justice investigation of police brutality charges "(*Miami Herald,* 6/16/80). The investigations were seen as a federal effort to help Miami "recover its ethnic equilibrium."

Establishment of Police Oversight Mechanisms

Reporting in 1980 described continued efforts to control the problem of police brutality. A June 28 (*Miami Herald,* 8/28/80) article described the Miami City Commission's creation of an Office of Professional Compliance to monitor the Miami Police Department's internal investigations. The Metro Public Safety Department also created an oversight panel.

In the words of one member of the new Metro Independent Review Panel, "In the post-McDuffie era, botched investigations are comparatively rare. . . . The police investigate themselves very well . . . They spend more time and do a better job investigating a complaint of rudeness against an officer than they do on an armed robbery. It's a sorry state that we've come to this, but I guess the public is demanding that the police be responsible. And they do a much better job knowing that we're going to review their work . . ." (*Miami Herald,* 12/30/80).

Police Use of Deadly Force: Policy Changes

July 28 (*Miami Herald,* 7/28/80) reporting described Miami and Metro (county) efforts to implement other brutality reforms including policy changes on police use of deadly force and on tactics of confrontation management, minority recruitment programs, stress control programs and psychological testing for police. Senator Daniel Scarborough and Representative Arnett Girardeau, both of Jacksonville, sought to impose strict limitations on the state's shoot-to-kill law. "Under the state's so-called Fleeing Felon Law which went into effect 10/1/75, police are permitted to kill a person suspected of a felony if the person runs" (*Florida Times-Union,* 4/27/80). Scarborough and Girardeau filed bills to restrict the use of deadly force by police to those situations where it is necessary to protect police officers and others from severe bodily injury or death. Representative Andy Johnson of Jacksonville co-sponsored the bill in the house.

Miami in Retrospect

Throughout the 1970s, about one-quarter of Miami's population was black. The Hispanic population, however, was about twice as large, constituting 45 percent of the population in 1970, and 56 percent at the end of the decade. Yet Miami papers reflect issues and problems of police brutality and disrespect toward blacks, and of black officers' exclusion from the Police Benevolent Association. While blacks were trying to establish greater accountability and control over the city police department, Hispanics were largely silent. The much publicized difficulties in the police/minority relationship were largely black problems.

In 1972 about one-third of the Miami Police Department's 800 officer force was black (*Miami Herald,* 11/9/72). As the city struggled to move forward in the midst of the region's strong historical bias against blacks, Hispanic demands for representation and protection either were not articulated or not picked up by the city's press. However, the city's lower than expected levels of police expenditures, especially in 1978, but to some extent in 1972 as well, may in part have resulted from the fact that the 81 percent minority population (68% in 1970) did not value the crime fighting abilities of police sufficiently to try to combat the city's extremely high crime rate with greater police appropriations. As discussed earlier in consideration of minority views of the police, crime is often seen as a fact of life in minority communities—serious and disturbing—but not easily rectified by the police, who therefore do not receive the highest priority in funding appropriations.

Implications

Overall, this update of five of the southern and western cities in the analysis further illustrates the importance of regional context and minority size on collective commitment to policing and on police/community relations. Miami, for example, reflected the tensions and biases of the South (1) in the Police Benevolent Association's continued refusal to admit blacks until all levels of the court system made it clear that such exclusion was discriminatory; (2) in the delayed militancy of the city's black population, as evidenced by the 1980 demonstrations and riot sparked by the McDuffie brutality trial verdict; and (3) in the continued focus on problems of black/white relations despite the fact that by the end of the decade over 50 percent of the city's population was Hispanic.

In Albuquerque, with 34 percent Hispanic and 2 percent black, police spending, especially capital expenditures, remained considerably higher than expected in 1978, despite the end of federal funding for capital police needs, and the national urban trend toward lower levels (after inflation) of spending in this area. Similarly, in Denver—12 percent black and 19 percent Hispanic—police spending for capital items increased enormously during the decade, as did police spending overall. At $11 per capita, Denver's capital police expenditures were close to five times the end-of-the-decade average for cities greater than 50,000 in population, even after much tension early in the decade between police and Denver's minority community.

Atlanta, a majority black southern city in 1978, spent about one-third less on capital items in 1978 than it did early in the decade, and its police expenditures overall were still under the expected level. Newspaper reports at the end of the decade indicate that blacks and whites were still competing for control of the police bureaucracy, but provide no evidence that other issues of dominance and control affect the city's social control agenda.

The City of Miami's police expenditures were increasingly underfinanced (in light of the city's socioeconomic characteristics) during the 1970s. No doubt the overlapping jurisdictional structure of Greater Miami played a role in keeping the City of Miami's totals to a minimum, but administrative overlaps cannot explain the increase in the deviation of city totals from expected police expenditure levels. It is likely that the growing minority population of the city became increasingly weary (as did the press) of police failures in race relations, and saw little prospect for reducing crime by allocating greater resources to the police.

Finally, San Francisco presents a picture of transition that is probably most reflective of the influence of urban diversity on city police. Although 1972 reporting contains some references to racial bias in police behavior and deployment, by the end of the decade Hispanics, Asians, American Indians (all "emerging minorities" in the federal government's terms), and women figured importantly in the city's police officer recruitment drive, and charges of police brutality came from gays, not blacks or Hispanics. Police spending remained under expected levels in the city throughout the decade. This is not surprising, as reporting in San Francisco focused on increasing the community relations skills of the force, and on hiring to make the force reflective of the diversity of the city's population.

Overall, we see in these cities trends reflecting the findings of the national study: (1) the continued (but without escalation) salience of race in police work and recruitment efforts; (2) the continued importance of region as a contextual demarcator influencing the salience of racial and ethnic divisions on police work; and (3) the increasing importance of the "emerging" minorities—Hispanics, Asians, American Indians, gays—on police activity and police force composition. In the next chapter we will assess the overall influence of social conflict on social control resource allocation and summarize the results of the national and individual city analyses.

8

Policing, Minorities, and Social Context: Conclusions and Implications

In assessing the link between minority group threat, crime, and policing, this investigation has focused on the determinants of police resource allocations in cities throughout the United States. While some of these determinants (city population size, density, and the crime rate, for example) were predicted by accepted theory and past research, others, such as the relative size of black and Hispanic population groups, percent poor, and black/white income inequality, were not expected on the basis of the traditional theoretical frameworks. The influence of these newly recognized determinants is best interpreted, in part, as a consequence of intergroup conflict, an element ignored until recently in models of collective commitment to formal social control efforts.

Previous research has provided some evidence that minority size influences majority hostility. Among white southerners, for example, prejudice has been found to be associated with percent black in the county (Giles, 1977). In addition, whites see themselves as having less power where the relative size of the minority population is larger. [Black self-estimates of power, however, do not vary with the proportion black in the population (Evans and Giles, 1986).] As noted in Chapter 1, it appears that members of the majority group are more sensitive to social disorganization, cultural differences, and sociopolitical dominance questions when the subordinate minority group is larger.

ETHNIC ANTAGONISM AND THE MOBILIZATION OF POLICE RESOURCES

The influence of minority size on social control efforts is not peculiar to the United States. Recent work on ethnic antagonism toward foreign workers in Switzerland indicates that the degree of public concern over the presence of "foreign elements" in the population increases with the size of the group. Wallimann (1984) describes the situation in Switzerland, where majority group concern over the presence of foreign elements is rooted in fear of loss of cultural heritage, identity, and the traditional way of life. Fear and its associated antagonism toward foreign elements are greatest among those closest to the structurally disadvantaged in economic resources, educational achievement, and geographic proximity.

Exclusion efforts and discrimination toward foreign workers increase with their number. In Switzerland, demands for exclusion and pressure to deny full citizenship—voting rights, home ownership, the right of family in-migration—arise periodically when " 'foreign elements' are believed to be getting too strong in various ways" (a situation referred to as "ueberfremdung") (Wallimann, 1984: 158). Since the juxtaposition of economic, racial, and ethnic groups in the United States varies by region, city size, and time period, it is not surprising that social context influences the minority group size/social control relationship.

City Size

Large city size appears to escalate the degree of black threat. Early in the 1970s the impact of percent black on municipal police appropriations was positive and significant in cities of 50,000 or more, while it was negligible in small cities—despite the multivariate equation and the similarity in the average percentage and the degree of variation in the size of the minority population in the two groups of cities. Furthermore, in large cities the percent black/capital expenditures relationship formed a curve similar in shape to the threat curve described by Blalock—increasing in slope until blacks constitute a majority of the population and declining after that. The link between interracial tension and municipal police departments' buildup of anti-riot gear alluded to by others (cf. Button, 1978; Feagin and Hahn, 1973) is a likely explanation for this pattern.

The threat curve was not detected in small cities. That finding and the general lack of significance of the impact of percent black on police appropriations in small cities suggest that the black population is perceived as a greater threat in large cities. It may be that in large cities greater anonymity and weaker informal social control exacerbate fear of crime and loss of dominance. The tighter social fabric of smaller cities—that is, their higher levels of social cohesion and greater capacity for informal social control and surveillance—may make it less likely that a large black population triggers greater municipal commitment to law enforcement.

Region

The impact of minority size on the level of public fiscal commitment to policing is also influenced by regional context, which varies in population composition, stratification patterns, history of minority/majority relations, level of prosperity, and forecast for economic growth. Overall, the evidence suggests that the racial and ethnic stratification system characteristic of a region is an important backdrop for minority size, influencing the extent to which it triggers public support for city police.

As expected, given the history of black/white relations in the South, the impact of percent black on capital police expenditures early in the decade was greater, and the threat curve more pronounced in the large cities of the South than in large cities generally. The degree of influence of the relative size of the Hispanic population on police expenditures also varied regionally. Early in the decade its influence was negligible in cities of the Northeast and North Central regions, while it was both positive and significant in southern and southwestern cities. In the South and Southwest, however, the percent Hispanic/capital expenditures relationship formed a threat curve similar to that formed by the percent black/capital expenditures relationship.

Temporal Proximity to Racial Strife

Funding for police equipment purchases by the Law Enforcement Assistance Administration in the early 1970s has been criticized by many for having exacerbated the minority/majority hostility that was a legacy of the 1960s (cf. Feagin and Hahn, 1973; Feeley and Sarat, 1980; Michalowski, 1985). Considerable evidence suggests that during the 1970s there was a general backing away from national attention to municipal law enforcement efforts relating to race and ethnicity (cf. Button, 1978). The results reported here indicate that as federal funding for riot training and equipment for police trickled to a halt, the impact of minority size on city spending for capital police items, which in 1971 had been best depicted by Blalock's (1967) threat curve, also disappeared.

In general, at the end of the decade, percent black still influenced municipal police expenditures. The impact of percent Hispanic increased somewhat, especially in the western and southern cities subpopulation, where its relationship with expenditures for police salaries and operations formed a threat curve. The shift in national attention from blacks to other "emerging" minorities may have contributed to perceptions of Hispanic threat. And, the federal government's movement away from providing fiscal support for quasi-military preparations to contain racial strife may have left cities on their own in setting priorities for capital expenditures, possibly accounting for reductions in the model's effectiveness in predicting 1978 expenditure levels.

POLICE/MINORITY ISSUES AT THE END OF THE DECADE

The late 1970s were difficult for municipal police departments in the United States. They were under siege by blacks, Hispanic groups, and females on three fronts: (1) brutality and misconduct toward minority groups and women, (2) hiring biases resulting in underrepresentation of minorities and women on the force, (3) discrimination in assignments and promotions with little minority or female representation at the higher ranks. In the midst of public pressure to address these issues, significant police layoffs, often of 200 or so officers, were implemented.

Certainly the major cutback in federal law and order funds to cities had settled in by the end of the decade, but the massive police layoffs implemented in Newark, Detroit, Philadelphia, and even Chicago were not accompanied by municipal efforts to increase revenues through taxation or to maintain current levels of police strength at the expense of other city services—both common strategies in earlier years. Rather, what emerged clearly in several cities was a general recognition of the fact that while crime is a serious liability of municipal life, police do not control its level. Quotations from public officials in Newark, Detroit, Chicago, and Philadelphia reflect this view in varying degrees, ranging from Newark Mayor Gibson's comments that the public has been sold a "bill of goods" about the need for police officers, to Chicago Mayor Byrne's less direct statements underscoring the need to increase police efficiency and decrease graft within police operations.

Police Accountability: Efforts to Curtail Brutality

Overall, these changes carved out a new role for urban police, a role in which accountability became a key word in serving the community. For example, early in his administration, Philadelphia's Police Commissioner Solomon required that every police officer be "a community relations officer" (*Philadelphia Inquirer,* 1/13/80). "The police department," he continued, "is one of the agencies in the City of Philadelphia that works twenty-four hours a day, seven days a week. . . . I want to start building up a mutual respect between the people of Philadelphia and the police department. . . . the best way to do it is to let everyone know that policemen are their friends." In the wake of the U.S. Justice Department's initiation of a lawsuit alleging willful and consistent brutality by the Philadelphia Police Department, Commissioner Solomon cracked down on physical and verbal abuse of citizens by police officers, suspending and firing officers when necessary, and indicating publicly that officers who violate police procedures regarding physical and deadly force were no better than common criminals and would be punished with the full weight of the law (*Evening Bulletin,* 9/2/80, 8/31/80, 2/26/80).

Another illustration of the importance of police accountability at the end of the decade can be found in Chicago, where Mayor Byrne named a Citizen's Committee to investigate the extent of police brutality in the city, indicating that she was "troubled by recurring reports in the news media about police brutality" (*Chicago Tribune,* 9/24/80). The *Chicago Tribune* (9/24/80) quoted her resolve to ". . . get to the bottom of these charges . . . [and that] one [case] is too much." The president of the Chicago Police Board, Reverend Wilbur Daniel, hailed the formation of the Committee as "long overdue." In his words, "The police are there to serve and protect and not to abuse, and abuse of powers has happened and is happening. [He] commended the mayor and . . . [vowed to] work vigorously with the committee to get the police department to where it should be" (*Daily Defender,* 9/24/80).

Detroit, seemingly further ahead than other cities in terms of police accountability (given its civilian police commission), witnessed city council demands for a crackdown on police brutality and misconduct (*Detroit Free Press,* 5/9/80). A later article in the *Detroit Free Press* (8/11/80) describing a "typical" police precinct in the city noted that while "police admit that most of their hostile confrontations with residents occur in poor, black neighborhoods . . . the . . . Precinct has shed its reputation as a hostile white bastion explosively at odds with the surrounding community. About 50 percent of the police . . . are black . . . and [there is now] a strong emphasis on community relations. . . ."

In 1979, Wichita was also among the cities where police brutality—and efforts to end it—were on the public agenda. Allegations of brutality and excessive use of force (*Wichita Eagle,* 1/18/79a, 1/18/79b, 1/19/79), public hearings on the subject (*Wichita Eagle,* 2/16/79), studies and analyses of the problem (*Wichita Eagle,* 6/24/79, 6/25/79, 6/27/79, 6/28/79) were daily news. Central to the discussion was the new emphasis on police accountability. One article indicated that police officers "fear that getting involved in a controversial situation with a black could cost them their jobs . . ." (*Wichita Eagle,* 6/27/79). Discussion of a proposal to create a citizen complaint screening board surfaced in May (*Wichita Eagle,* 5/2/79); this group would "receive complaints and make sufficient investigation to determine if the complaints have merit."

Similarly, the Miami City Commission established an Office of Professional Compliance in July 1980, although it was still not in place by December (*Miami Herald,* 12/30/80). The new office, within the Miami Police Department, was intended to oversee internal investigation and to report directly to the chief of police. In addition, the department began tracking the number of citizen complaints against each officer, creating a "five-plus" list of officers with five or more complaints in a two-year period—"whether the complaints are substantiated or not. . . . Officers who tend to draw complaints from citizens, or who use force or discharge their weapons frequently, get special counseling . . . " (*Miami Herald,* 12/30/80).

The *Miami Herald* at the end of the decade was full of the facts and figures of police brutality, indicating, for example, that "most brutality claimants are white. But blacks who make up about a fifth of the local population file a disproportionate third of the brutality claims" (*Miami Herald,* 7/22/79). In an article analyzing the situation entitled, "Police Operate in a World of Hostility" (*Miami Herald,* 7/25/79a), a white Miami patrolman's view was quoted: "No doubt about it, the job makes you more racist. Not in a one-on-one situation. But when I'm having to deal with a crowd of blacks, they're the enemy. I'm not the good guy to them. I'm the white establishment. . . ."

A black patrolman implicated in instances of police brutality gave his perspective: "Whatever group you have the most of dominates the running of the department. That's what we've got now—a department run by white values." But the paper editorialized, "a principle of minimum force crosses racial lines . . . [a] policy that an officer should use no more force than necessary. Even police officers who get swept away in a moment of emotion recognize it. Those who violate it sometimes suffer the consequences" (*Miami Herald,* 7/25/79a).

Police Use of Deadly Force

Another prevalent theme in end-of-the-decade municipal news reporting is the movement to limit police use of deadly force. In Miami, for example, a new policy on when to use deadly force took effect two days after the McDuffie riot (May 17-19, 1980), although the policy change had been in preparation for two years. The new policy ruled out the use of deadly force unless: ". . . a fleeing suspect has just caused death or great bodily harm . . . a fleeing suspect has just committed a felony and is armed and dangerous. . . . the suspect is placing an officer or a citizen in immediate danger of death or great bodily harm." Use of a gun was ruled out in many situations in which it would have been permitted by Florida's "fleeing felon" law (*Miami Herald,* 7/28/80). Assistant Miami Police Chief Michael Cosgrove explained that "The vast majority of disturbances that have occurred throughout this country [since the 1960s] . . . have been precipitated by police use of deadly force on unarmed civilian persons that have been involved in property offenses. The trend throughout the country right now is to shore up these areas" (*Miami Herald,* 7/28/80).

In Philadelphia, a similar tightening of police policy on deadly force was put into effect at the end of April 1980 (*Philadelphia Inquirer,* 4/20/80), requiring that an officer know (not merely believe) that a fleeing suspect is armed, has used the weapon, or is about to use it. Police officers were issued wallet cards on which the directive was printed. And in July, a police officer was suspended for a May 29 shooting that was in violation of the deadly force rules (*Evening Bulletin,* 7/2/80). As the Fraternal Order of Police in Philadelphia filed suit in court to block the directive, the *Evening Bulletin* (10/9/80) looked at the "deadly force" rules in some other cities, finding that "of the 10 largest U.S. cities, New York, Los Angeles, Houston, Detroit, and San Antonio, Texas, have tougher rules against an officer shooting at a person escaping from a felony. Regulations in Chicago, Dallas, Baltimore and San Diego are about the same as those developed by Philadelphia's Green Administration."

A new policy regulating firearm use by Wichita police officers was adopted in June 1980. Establishment of the policy capped months of debate on police firearm use in the city, and considerable journalistic investigation and discussion of the extent and determinants of police brutality toward the city's blacks. More restrictive than their precedents, the new rules permitted officers to shoot at suspects only if they are armed, have threatened, or are threatening to kill or greatly injure police or citizens. State law at the time was more liberal, allowing "officers to shoot at persons involved in any felony" (*Wichita Eagle,* 1/15/80).

Wichita's new restrictions were recommended by the Police Firearms Evaluation Committee in November, as was "the newly adopted provision that officers not shoot at occupants of a vehicle unless citizens or police . . . [were] threatened with deadly force" (*Wichita Eagle,* 1/15/80). The new policy also prohibited the use of automatic firearms, and set guidelines for the type of ammunition permissible. The president of Wichita's chapter of the American Civil Liberties Union praised the new policy, but pushed for a change in the state law, so that violation of the policy would become a criminal offense, rather than merely a departmental policy violation.

Police Officer Stress

Along with the effort to understand police brutality and to make every police officer a community relations officer came a greater understanding of stress as a major liability of police work. A Wichita patrol officer warned, for example, that "you have to remember that nobody's perfect, but everybody demands that cops not be fallible human beings" (*Wichita Eagle,* 6/27/79). On the basis of interviews with several officers and supervisors, the *Wichita Eagle* described police as "people with good intentions whose alienation from the society they serve has helped them justify many incidents that would horrify an observer" (*Wichita Eagle,* 6/27/79).

Explaining the officers' views that mistakes, overreactions, or displays of temper usually surface "during extremely stressful situations," the paper cited Wichita Police Chief Richard LaMunyon's view that the "factors creating that stress can range from being under pistol fire to being thrown out of the house by a spouse before coming to work . . . divorce rates for officers are higher than for most other groups." LaMunyon continued:

It's not fair, but nobody said the job was going to be fair. Police officers are expected to hit people, but you're not supposed to bleed. They are not supposed to show emotion when they scrape up some little baby that has been run over in the street. That all builds up in the officers.

This is how they perceive their role: Everything's out of control, but I've got to remain in control. In reality, everything's really churning inside, emotionally churning . . . (*Wichita Eagle,* 6/27/79).

The officer quickly becomes alienated from society, the *Wichita Eagle* (6/27/79) reports, expected to "spend every day working in the sewer with scum. . . ." A lieutenant with the Organized Crime Unit explained that "early in his career the officer is likely to develop a 'we versus them' attitude. 'We' is the cops. 'Them' is everybody else."

In San Francisco a three-year study of 267 police officers, completed in November 1980 for the city police commission, recommended that "prevention and treatment of stress be given the highest priority by the (police) department and the city" (*Oakland Tribune,* 11/20/80). In an article titled "Study Urges Stress Treatment for Police Officers," San Francisco Police Department training consultant and study director Mimi H. Silbert was quoted as saying that its "results . . . are alarming, the amount of stress experienced by officers is significant, and even more significant when it is noted that the longer the officers stay on the job, the less work satisfaction they have" (*Oakland Tribune,* 11/20/80).

According to Silbert job stress is of paramount concern to police officers today:

> The vast majority of the officers sampled stated that being a police officer creates stress for them at work . . . and almost half of the officers sampled said that being a police officer creates stress for them at home.
> Considering the fact that the officers surveyed [had] all been on the job only one to five years, these were extremely disturbing results (*Oakland Tribune,* 11/20/80).

The level of stress is influenced, Silbert explained, by the "low pay, paperwork and red tape, physical danger, inadequate tangible rewards and a lack of appreciation for performance." The report indicated that anxiety and exhaustion were "the major contributors to job burnout. . . . Hopelessness and feelings of rejection and worthlessness were the least significant." Symptoms of stress included "headaches, tenseness, back aches, nervousness, stomach aches, loss of appetite on duty, sleeping problems and nightmares . . ." (*Oakland Tribune,* 11/20/80).

Atlanta's 1980 five-year plan to "reshape" the police force included as a specific step provision for "employing a full-time staff psychologist for police officers," to be requested as part of the 1981 budget (*Atlanta Journal,* 5/16/80). In Miami the links between police officer stress and brutality were under public discussion. *Miami Herald* reporters rode for 140 hours through 15 full shifts with Miami area police. An article explaining that "Police Operate in World of Hostility" (*Miami Herald,* 7/25/79a), summarized the view that "letting it get to you can lead to brutality." In the words of a Miami police officer, "Guys do one of three things when they've been out here a while, when they realize they really can't do anything in court. . . . One, they retire out here and don't do nothin. Two, they quit the force. And three, they get violent" (*Miami Herald,* 7/25/79b).

The *Herald,* in an article entitled "Stress of Job Makes Some Turn to Brutality" (*Miami Herald,* 7/25/79b), quoted the view of Dr. Mark Axelberd of the Counseling and Stress Control Center in Coral Gables:

not all cases of police brutality can be blamed on stress. But it has real impact on police behavior. . . . [The officer] is a little too quick to make the arrest, a little too quick to use force . . . Very many investigations of excessive-force complaints show that the officers were in a state of desperation and frustration at the time. . . .

After some highly publicized incidents of brutality, including the police beating death of Arthur McDuffie, the Miami Metro Public Safety Department required that all officers pass a "valid and relevant psychological test" (*Miami Herald*, 1/9/80). Dr. Axelberd and Dr. Jose Valle won the contract to prepare and administer the tests until an examination under development at the University of Florida was completed. The test consisted of a four-hour battery of standard examinations, including the Minnesota Multiphasic Personality Inventory (MMPI), as a screen for pathology; the Beta Intelligence Test, as a measure of IQ; and the Strong Campbell Interest Test to compare the trainees' interests with those of police officers in general.

An article describing the results was headlined: "Psychologist Would Fire Most of Class" (*Miami Herald*, 9/21/80). After testing all 39 of the Metro police candidates in training, the psychologist recommended that up to 70 percent be dismissed as unfit to be police officers. In additon "as many as 30 percent of the 45 experienced officers who recently have left other departments to join the Dade Public Safety Department . . . failed the psychological exam. . . ; . . . low intelligence, signs of personality disorder, or vocational interest sharply dissimilar to other police officers . . ." led to recommendations for dismissal (*Miami Herald*, 9/21/80).

LINKING RACIAL AND ECONOMIC INEQUALITY TO SOCIAL CONTROL RESOURCE DETERMINATION

Recent study of the relationship between intergroup antagonism and police resource mobilization has helped clarify the determinants of both. Mobilization and deployment of police resources are triggered in part by intergroup conflict, not only in terms of violent demonstration and protest, but also in the form of less obvious threats to the prevailing cultural heritage, lifestyle, and distribution of economic power (employment opportunities as well as real wealth). In U.S. cities, fear of the loss of majority cultural identity may be a catalyst for both racial/ethnic antagonism and the mobilization of social control efforts, as it has been demonstrated to be in other nations (cf. Wallimann, 1984).

In the same way that the term minority is now understood to encompass a broad array of groups in the United States—blacks, Hispanics, Asians and (as the San Francisco Police Department's 1979 recruiting drive indicated) gays—so must the "majority" be seen to be a multifaceted group. It includes, for example, the white poor and the white working class, who, because of their economic situation, are likely to reside in communities that put them at greatest risk of street crime and the losses it entails. Collective mobilization of police resources might be stimulated in part by pressure from this facet of the majority for police crime control efforts. More affluent whites, on the other hand, typically reside at some distance from street crime and may be less personally affected by it. They may seek to safeguard their interests by pressing lawmakers for a legal code that protects their economic advantages (cf. Liska and Chamlin, 1984). Thus, economic cleavages within the majority yield different focal points for their pressure on the system of formal social control.

As Figure 1.1 suggests, the incorporation of insights derived from conflict theory into the models describing the determinants of collective commitment to social control has led to a broader understanding of the social structural and contextual variations on crime control. While these models were initially derived from rational economic production theory and consensus theory, a new, more complicated understanding has developed, one that clarifies what were initially relatively simplistic propositions regarding dominant group control of the legal system.

The new model looks not at control efforts by a single economically and politically dominant group, but rather portrays factions at varying levels of structural advantage—ethnic/racial, economic, and political—seeking to influence differing layers of social control authorities for protection of cultural, economic, political and social advantages (cf. Jackson, forthcoming). The allocation of social control resources is now seen to be influenced by minority group threat, fear of crime, competition for sociopolitical dominance, protection of cultural identity, social disorganization, inequality, poverty, and minority group size—not only through their influence on reported crime. In addition, contextual factors associated with region, city size, and temporal proximity to racial strife are understood to provide an important backdrop for interaction of the elements depicted in the model.

Investigation of the public view of the police provided additional evidence of the multifaceted nature of the minority population, at least in terms of ethnic antagonism, perceived minority threat, and police department response. Taking social context into consideration, especially in the form of region and time period, led to recognition of distinctions in the focus of perceptions of minority threat and the police role in relation to it. While blacks were in the forefront of police-related concerns in much of the nation early in the 1970s, Hispanics even then more often made the news in the western and southwestern cities investigated. This pattern was reinforced during the decade, with Hispanic/Anglo relations a greater concern in the West and Southwest in the late 1970s than in the beginning.

NEW EXPECTATIONS FOR POLICING

In all regions the expected police role in the community and the pattern of their interaction with members of minority groups changed noticeably during the decade. Early in the decade it was clear that the public expected the police to control crime. Reducing crime rates and maintaining order in cities were seen as jobs for the police. Where the job was not getting done, there were calls for more police (see, for example, *Philadelphia Inquirer,* 6/25/72; *Sun,* 5/29/72; *Albuquerque Journal,* 5/25/72; *Denver Post,* 1/16/72). While police brutality toward citizens was not condoned, "aggressive preventive patrol" practices were (cf. *Chicago Tribune,* 5/13/72), although they engendered resentment and complaints from minority group members.

By the end of the decade a new emphasis on police accountability, curbs on police use of deadly force, and an emerging understanding that social programs, not police, are needed to reduce crime all worked toward restructuring the police officer's role in the community. Expectations regarding his/her interactions with minority individuals and groups were changing. The stresses associated with police work—and their links to conflicting expectations and standards for police behavior—were explicitly examined in news reporting in several major cities. If newspaper coverage in major cities is any guide, by the end of the 1970s we had begun as a society to draw back from a law-and-order response to ethnic antagonism. We had begun to examine carefully the conflicts associated with policing in U.S. cities and move toward restructuring our expectations of the role of police and standards for police work.

The results of the national quantitative analysis support this view. They indicate by the end of the decade a considerably weakened impact of minority population composition in determining municipal appropriations for capital police expenditures, and an end to the threat curve that in 1971 depicted the minority size/capital police expenditures relationships. Both nationally and locally, we emerged from the 1970s ready to think about innovative approaches to policing American cities. Work by Skolnick and Bayley (1986) illustrates efforts toward this end by some major metropolitan police departments. Many of these efforts were small in scale, begun with little investment or commitment on the part of rank and file officers. Their success over time remains to be demonstrated. More importantly, however, public reconceptualization of the police role must continue in the forefront of discussion enlightened by realistic appraisal of the social and economic conditions of U.S. cities.

Appendix: Tables A.1–A.10

Table A.1
Zero Order Correlation Matrix with Means and Standard Deviations for All Cities, Large Cities, and Small Cities, 1970 and 1980

City Characteristics		1 (1970)	1 (1980)	2 (1970)	2 (1980)	3 (1970)	3 (1980)	4 (1970)	4 (1980)	5 (1970)	5 (1980)	6 (1970)	6 (1980)	7 (1970)	7 (1980)	8 (1970)	8 (1980)	9 (1970)	9 (1980)	10 (1970)	10 (1980)	X̄ (1970)	X̄ (1980)	S.D. (1970)	S.D. (1980)
1. Total Expenditures for Police	(A) All Cities*	—	—	.99c	.98	.42c	.30c	.52c	.36c	.34c	.30c	.44c	.19c	.06	.22c	.65c	.44c	.13b	-.05	.60c	.46c	24.43	44.49	11.40	18.82
	(B) Cities ≥ 50,000***	—	—	.99c	.98	.46c	.29c	.52c	.34c	.39c	.40c	.46c	.17c	.05	.36c	.67c	.46c	.10a	-.10	.61c	.53c	26.26	47.82	12.50	19.66
	(C) Cities < 50,000 and ≥ 25,000****	—	—	.99c	.99	.36c	.24	.43c	.34	.16a	.19	.06	.05	-.28a	-.04	.53c	.31	.22a	-.03	.52	.25	21.23	37.91	8.27	15.05
2. Salaries and Operations	A			—	—	.32c	.12b	.53c	.38c	.33c	.30c	.43c	.19c	-.07	.22c	.65c	.45c	.14	-.07	.60c	.45c	23.55	42.52	10.93	18.11
	B			—	—	.38c	.09a	.53c	.36c	.38c	.38c	.45c	.18c	.04	.35c	.66c	.47c	.22	-.12a	.60c	.53c	25.28	45.52	12.02	18.92
	C			—	—	.20a	.11	.46c	.36	.16	.20b	.06	.04	-.30c	-.04	.55c	.31c	.24b	.02	.52c	.25c	20.53	36.58	7.87	14.71
3. Capital Expenditures	A					—	—	.08	-.02	.19a	.05	.23b	.02	.08	.06	.24b	.05	-.05	.08a	.28b	.11b	.87	1.97	1.25	3.36
	B					—	—	.11a	-.04	.27b	.08	.30c	-.01	.15	.09	.33c	.02	-.07	.07	.31c	.12a	.98	2.30	1.14	3.84
	C					—	—	-.03	-.07	.05	-.01	-.01	-.04	.02	.01	.05	.08	.07	.11	.19a	.05	.69	1.33	1.42	1.94
4. Density	A							—	—	.12a	.11b	.33c	.26c	-.11a	.16c	.39c	.20c	.30c	.12c	.26b	.06	4.82	4.24	4.07	3.47
	B							—	—	.12a	.11a	.33c	.26c	-.04	.23c	.42c	.25c	.29c	.08	.25b	.04	5288.45	4.65	4619.56	3.85
	C							—	—	.09	.21b	-.06	.00	-.28b	.01	.20a	.12	.41c	.21b	.17a	.07	3990.63	3.45	2690.30	2.37
5. Per Cent Black	A									—	—	.15b	.10a	.63c	.69c	.17c	.16c	.00	-.08b	.25b	.11b	13.87	15.21	13.66	16.78
	B									—	—	.16b	.15b	.72c	.72c	.20a	.26c	-.11b	-.08	.26b	.12a	14.79	14.05	14.15	16.67
	C									—	—	-.02	-.03	.51c	.64c	.06	-.03	.24b	.05	.04	.12	12.25	17.51	13.66	16.80
6. Population Size	A											—	—	.05	.12b	.32c	.32c					152.25	127.35	456.35	363.06
	B											—	—	.08	.17c	.34c	.35c					21869.05	172.94	561965.32	438.59
	C											—	—	-.05	-.02	.19a	.03					36290.11	37.13	7069.41	6.58
7. Per Cent Poor	A													—	—	-.06	.18c	.18a	-.09a	.21a	.44c	10.09	10.30	4.74	5.33
	B													—	—	-.03	.26c	.17c	-.11a	.32c	.48c	9.93	9.94	4.44	5.43
	C													—	—	-.11	-.03	.22a	-.08	.08	.39c	10.36	11.02	5.23	5.07
8. Per Capital City Revenue	A															—	—	-.44c	-.25c	.31c	.23c	181.50	520.97	116.45	290.77
	B															—	—	-.44c	-.22c	.32c	.26c	195.30	551.37	125.16	306.72
	C															—	—	-.46c	-.33c	.19a	.14a	157.42	460.82	95.09	246.20
9. Black/White Median Income	A																	—	—	-.00	-.24c	.68	.72	.16	.22
	B																	—	—	-.02	-.28c	.67	.72	.15	.23
	C																	—	—	.04	-.17a	.68	.70	.17	.19
10. Crime Rate	A																			—	—	31.46	79.63	14.44	26.23
	B																			—	—	34.10	81.08	14.65	26.57
	C																			—	—	26.84	76.75	12.87	25.34

*(A)   1970 N=442   1980 N=566

**(B)   1970 N=281   1980 N=376

***(C)   1970 N=161   1980 N=190

ᵃp<.05   ᵇp<.01   ᶜp<.001

Table A.2
Impact of Percent Black and Other City Characteristics on Policing Expenditures in Cities ≥ 25,000 Population: Regression Results

	Total Expenditures for Police				Salaries and Operations				Capital Expenditures			
	Linear Model		Nonlinear Model		Linear Model		Nonlinear Model		Linear Model		Nonlinear Model	
	1970	1980	1970	1980	1970	1980	1970	1980	1970	1980	1970	1980
Constant	11.911	6.233	10.473	7.021	11.597	7.172	10.245	7.815	.314	-.533	.230	.484
Population Size												
S	.166[c]	-.021	.161[c]	-.020	.155[c]	-.025	.151[c]	-.024	.153[b]	.026	.146[b]	.024
U	.000	-.001	.000	-.001	.000	-.001	.003	-.001	.000	.000	.000	.000
SE	.000	.002	.000	.002	.000	.002	.000	.002	.000	.000	.000	.000
Density												
S	.223[c]	.287[c]	.226[c]	.286[c]	.243[c]	.310[c]	.246[c]	.308[c]	-.708	-.092[b]	-.076	-.089[a]
U	.001	.002	.001	.002	.001	.002	.001	.002	.000	.000	.000	.000
SE	.000	.000	.000	.000	.000	.000	.000	.000	.000	.000	.000	.000
Per Cent Black												
S	.182[c]	.191[c]	.461[b]	.103	.181[c]	.196[c]	.478[c]	.141	.071	.029	.076	-.094
U	.141	.214	.359	.166	.134	.212	.355	.152	.006	.005	.007	-.107
SE	.030	.051	.129	.197	.028	.049	.123	.187	.006	.011	.025	.042
Black/White Median Income												
S	-.042	.044	-.033	.039	-.039	.021	-.030	.016	-.042	.128[c]	-.037	.129[c]
U	-2.788	3.884	-2.178	3.392	-2.439	1.796	-1.900	1.345	-.355	1.858	-.296	1.872
SE	2.108	3.016	2.136	3.137	2.002	2.865	2.027	2.980	.421	.647	.427	.672
Per Cent Poor												
S	-.247[c]	-.168[c]	-.240[c]	-.170[c]	-.255[c]	-.180[c]	-.249[c]	-.183[c]	-.024	-.038	-.022	.041
U	-.544	-.583	-.527	-.600	-.537	-.612	-.522	-.621	-.006	-.022	-.006	.024
SE	.083	.163	.084	.164	.079	.155	.079	.156	.017	.035	.017	.035
Per Capita City Revenue												
S	.326[c]	.307[c]	.328[c]	.307[c]	.321[c]	.313[c]	.324[c]	.314[c]	.159[b]	.048	.170[b]	.045
U	.031	.020	.031	.020	.029	.020	.029	.020	.002	.000	.002	.000
SE	.003	.002	.003	.002	.003	.002	.003	.002	.001	.000	.001	.000
Crime Rate												
S	.398[c]	.377[c]	.384[c]	.378[c]	.385[c]	.369[c]	.380[c]	.371[c]	.183[c]	.098[c]	.184[c]	.096[a]
U	.284	.270	.280	.272	.268	.255	.264	.256	.016	.011	.016	.011
SE	.023	.026	.023	.027	.022	.015	.022	.026	.005	.005	.005	.005
(Per Cent Black)²												
S	—	—	-.511	.103	—	—	-.570	.068	—	—	.179	.368
U			-.084	.116			-.090	.001			.000	.001
SE			.058	.197			.055	.006			.001	.001
(Per Cent Black)³												
S	—	—	.241	-.071	—	—	.286	-.010	—	—	-.211[a]	-.275
U			.000	.000			.000	-.003			.000	.000
SE			.000	.000			.000	.056			.000	.000
R^2	.687[c]	.425[c]	.690[c]	.426[c]	.691[c]	.440[c]	.693[c]	.441[c]	.132[c]	.032	.135[c]	.034

[a] p(for one-tailed test)<.05 [b] p<.01 [c] p<.001

Table A.3
Impact of Percent Black and Other City Characteristics on Policing Expenditures in Cities ≥ 50,000 Population: Regression Results

	Total Expenditures for Police				Salaries and Operations				Capital Expenditures			
	Linear Model		Nonlinear Model		Linear Model		Nonlinear Model		Linear Model		Nonlinear Model	
	1970	1980	1970	1980	1970	1980	1970	1980	1970	1980	1970	1980
Constant	11.970	3.128	10.780	4.892	11.577	3.902	10.170	5.644	.400	-.648	.604	-.685
Population Size												
Standardized (S)	.191[c]	-.048	.187[c]	-.045	.180[c]	-.049	.176[c]	-.046	.190[b]	.001	.188[b]	-.004
Unstandardized (U)	.000	-.002	.000	-.002	.000	-.002	.000	-.002	.000	.000	.000	.000
Standardized Error (SE)	.000	-.002	.001	.002	.000	-.002	.000	.002	.000	.000	.000	.000
Density												
S	.230[c]	.261[c]	.232[c]	.259[c]	.251[c]	.285[c]	.253[c]	.283[c]	-.097	-.112[a]	-.101	-.107[a]
U	.001	.001	.001	.001	.001	.001	.001	.001	.000	.000	.000	.000
SE	.000	.000	.095	.000	.000	.000	.000	.000	.000	.000	.000	.000
Per Cent Black												
S	.245[c]	.194[c]	.447[c]	-.109	.240[c]	.193[c]	.502[b]	-.100	.143[a]	.060	-.364	-.015
U	.199	.229	.362	.129	.186	.219	.389	-.113	.012	.013	.029	-.003
SE	.042	.067	.166	.246	.041	.063	.160	.234	.007	.016	.026	.059
Black/White Median Income												
S	-.036	.059	-.027	.046	-.031	.035	-.020	.021	-.055	.126[a]	-.071	.132[b]
U	-2.691	5.142	-1.983	4.029	-2.229	2.951	-1.427	1.772	-.417	1.978	-.540	2.075
SE	2.900	3.554	2.973	3.698	2.792	3.374	2.859	3.513	.481	.858	.489	.891
Per Cent Poor												
S	-.268[c]	-.101[a]	-.264[c]	-.098[a]	-.275[c]	-.114[a]	-.270[c]	-.113[a]	-.042	.051	-.506	.059
U	-.674	-.364	-.664	.355	-.660	-.396	-.649	-.394	-.011	.033	-.014	.039
SE	.131	.209	.132	.209	.127	.198	.127	.199	.022	.050	.021	.050
Per Capita City Revenue												
S	.306[c]	.277[c]	.305[c]	.277[c]	.294[c]	.289[c]	.293[c]	.291[c]	.241[c]	.027	.256[c]	.024
U	.029	.018	.029	.018	.027	.018	.027	.018	.002	.000	.002	.000
SE	.004	.003	.004	.003	.004	.003	.004	.003	.001	.000	.001	.001
Crime Rate												
S	.391[c]	.429[c]	.386[c]	.434[c]	.392[c]	.422[c]	.386[c]	.428[a]	.155[a]	.115[a]	.170[b]	.106[a]
U	.301	.318	.298	.320	.289	.300	.284	.305	.012	.015	.013	.014
SE	.030	.034	.030	.034	.029	.032	.029	.032	.005	.008	.005	.008
(Per Cent Black)²												
S	—	—	-.345	.650	—	—	.470	.597	—	—	1.187[a]	.345
U	—	—	-.006	.013	—	—	.008	.011	—	—	.002	.001
SE	—	—	.007	.008	—	—	.007	.008	—	—	.001	.002
(Per Cent Black)³												
S	—	—	.152	-.393	—	—	.220	.342	—	—	-.747[a]	-.311
U	—	—	.000	.000	—	—	.000	.000	—	—	.000	.000
SE	—	—	.000	.000	—	—	.000	.000	—	—	.000	.000
R^2	.704[c]	.469[c]	.705[c]	.473[c]	.700[c]	.483[c]	.702[c]	.486[c]	.211[c]	.043	.221[c]	.048

[a] p (for one-tailed test) <.05 [b] p<.01 [c] p<.001

131

Table A.4
Impact of Percent Black and Other City Characteristics on Policing Expenditures in Cities of 25,000-50,000 Population: Regression Results

	Total Expenditures for Police				Salaries and Operations				Capital Expenditures			
	Linear Model		Nonlinear Model		Linear Model		Nonlinear Model		Linear Model		Nonlinear Model	
	1970	1980	1970	1980	1970	1980	1970	1980	1970	1980	1970	1980
Constant	13.447	20.166	10.867	17.809	12.997	20.258	11.006	17.965	1.004	.659	.815	.653
Population Size												
S	-.016	.006	-.009	.006	-.011	.001	-.005	.002	-.086	-.012	-.083	.001
U	.001	.012	.001	.013	.000	.002	.000	.004	.000	-.002	.000	.000
SE	.000	.134	.000	.135	.000	.130	.000	.130	.000	.012	.000	.012
Density												
S	.228[c]	.302[c]	.243[c]	.299[c]	.253[c]	.326[c]	.264[c]	.322[c]	-.044	-.101	-.024	-.125
U	.001	.002	.001	.002	.001	.002	.001	.002	.000	.000	.000	.000
SE	.000	.000	.000	.000	.000	.000	.000	.000	.000	.000	.000	.000
Per Cent Black												
S	.098	.193[a]	.682	.445	.107[a]	.999[b]	.623[a]	.498	-.096	.079	.175	.350
U	.064	.163	.446	.377	.066	.166	.387	.414	-.005	.005	.008	.023
SE	.043	.071	.231	.352	.040	.069	.212	.341	.005	.006	.025	.030
Black/White Median Income												
S	-.078	-.008	-.074	.007	-.082	.031	-.079	-.016	-.155	.057	-.141	.041
U	-3.816	-.597	-3.601	.486	-3.818	-2.178	-3.704	-1.094	-.549	.337	-.501	.242
SE	3.161	4.970	3.151	5.152	2.892	4.816	2.893	4.991	.346	.475	.345	.490
Per Cent Poor												
S	-.294[c]	-.303[c]	-.271	-.292[c]	-.308[c]	-.312[c]	-.290[c]	-.301[c]	-.064	.061	-.031	.047
U	-.465	-.845	-.428	-.816	-.463	-.853	-.437	-.822	-.007	.013	-.004	.010
SE	.106	.236	.107	.239	.097	.229	.098	.232	.012	.022	.012	.022
Per Capita City Revenue												
S	.389[c]	.308[c]	.401[c]	.312[c]	.404[c]	.307[c]	.412[c]	.313[c]	.050	.074	.074	.078
U	.034	.017	.035	.017	.033	.017	.034	.018	.000	.000	.000	.000
SE	.005	.004	.005	.004	.004	.004	.004	.004	.001	.000	.001	.000
Crime Rate												
S	.404[c]	.229[c]	.400[c]	.227[c]	.388[c]	.226[c]	.386[c]	.224[c]	.275[c]	.028	.268[c]	.031
U	.260	.126	.257	.124	.237	.121	.235	.120	.013	.001	.013	.001
SE	.036	.039	.036	.039	.033	.037	.033	.037	.004	.003	.004	.003
(Per Cent Black)²												
S	—	—	-1.144	-.423	—	—	-1.071	-.536	—	—	-.108	-.937
U			-.160	-.006			-.143	-.007			.000	-.001
SE			.117	.013			.107	.013			.001	.001
(Per Cent Black)³												
S	—	—	.567	.171	—	—	.568	.241	—	—	.213	.743
U			.163	.000			.155	.000			.000	.000
SE			.152	.000			.140	.000			.112	.043
R²	.596[c]	.287[c]	.606[c]	.291[c]	.626[c]	.302[c]	.633[c]	.306[c]	.093	.031	.112	.043

[a] p(for one-tailed test)<.05
[b] p<.01
[c] p<.01

Table A.5
Impact of Percent Black and Other City Characteristics on Policing Expenditures in Southern Cities ≥ 50,000 Population: Regression Results

	Total Expenditures for Police				Salaries and Operations				Capital Expenditures			
	Linear Model		Nonlinear Model		Linear Model		Nonlinear Model		Linear Model		Nonlinear Model	
	1970	1980	1970	1980	1970	1980	1970	1980	1970	1980	1970	1980
Constant	11.740	2.749	10.057	8.429	11.633	6.587	9.641	8.065	-.197	1.882	.441	2.307
Population Size												
Standardized (S)	.069	.147[a]	.057	.138[a]	.057	.151[a]	.044	.141[a]	.121	-.013	.150	-.009
Unstandardized (U)	.000	.015	.000	.014	.000	.015	.002	.014	.000	.000	.000	.000
Standard Error (SE)	.000	.007	.000	.007	.000	.007	.003	.007	.000	.002	.000	.002
Density												
S	.373[c]	.386[c]	.360[c]	.396[c]	.364[c]	.394[c]	.351[c]	.402[c]	.305[b]	-.022	.380[c]	-.008
U	.002	.003	.002	.003	.002	.003	.002	.003	.000	.000	.000	.000
SE	.000	.000	.000	.000	.000	.001	.000	.000	.000	.000	.000	.000
Per Cent Black												
S	.264[b]	.345[a]	1.101[a]	.713	.262[a]	.292[c]	1.252[a]	.627	.191	.336[a]	-.830	.545
U	.167	.349	.698	.720	.150	.291	.720	.626	.015	.056	-.063	.093
SE	.070	.110	.391	.640	.066	.105	.362	.612	.013	.030	.050	.175
Black/White Median Income												
S	-.086	.072	-.086	.088	-.087	.045	-.085	.059	.033	.162	-.055	.179
U	-8.124	6.884	-8.127	8.449	-7.500	4.249	-7.273	5.544	.401	2.636	-.669	2.905
SE	7.536	8.365	7.783	9.011	6.998	8.006	7.198	8.621	1.302	2.287	1.308	2.466
Per Cent Poor												
S	-.246[b]	-.281[c]	-.253[b]	-.279[c]	-.245[b]	-.258[c]	-.254[b]	-.257[c]	-.142	-.153	-.172	-.145
U	-.481	-.908	-.496	-.899	-.434	-.824	-.450	-.819	-.035	-.084	-.043	-.080
SE	.187	.298	.198	.303	.174	.285	.173	.290	.033	.081	.032	.083
Per Capita City Revenue												
S	.223[b]	.121	.218[b]	.108[b]	.216[b]	.125[a]	.207[a]	.114	.086	-.018	.267[a]	-.028
U	.018	.007	.017	.006	.016	.007	.015	.007	.001	.000	.002	.000
SE	.007	.005	.007	.005	.007	.004	.007	.005	.001	.001	.001	.001
Crime Rate												
S	.334[c]	.442[c]	.333[c]	.432[c]	.347[c]	.465[c]	.344[c]	.456[c]	.150	-.104	.163	-.112
U	.234	.265	.233	.259	.221	.276	.219	.271	.013	-.011	.013	-.011
SE	.056	.043	.057	.045	.052	.041	.052	.043	.010	.012	.010	.012
(Per Cent Black)²												
S	—	—	-2.083	-.807	—	—	-2.416[a]	-.773	—	—	2.715[a]	-.252
U			.027	-.015			.028	-.014			.004	-.001
SE			.018	.024			.016	.023			.002	.006
(Per Cent Black)³												
S	—	—	1.315	.482	—	—	1.505[a]	.479	—	—	-2.024[c]	.047
U			.000	.000			.000	.000			.000	.000
SE			.000	.000			.000	.000			.000	.000
R²	.697[c]	.635[c]	.706[c]	.637[c]	.683[c]	.658[c]	.695[c]	.660[c]	.406[c]	.055	.477[c]	.057

[a]p(for one-tailed test)<.05   [b]p<.01   [c]p<.001

133

Table A.6
Impact of Percent Black and Other City Characteristics on Policing Expenditures in Southern Cities of 25,000-50,000 Population: Regression Results

	Total Expenditures for Police				Salaries and Operations				Capital Expenditures			
	Linear Model		Nonlinear Model		Linear Model		Nonlinear Model		Linear Model		Nonlinear Model	
	1970	1980	1970	1980	1970	1980	1970	1980	1970	1980	1970	1980
Constant	15.564	14.198	16.920	26.008	16.010	12.802	17.568	25.193	-.466	1.396	-.648	.816
Population Size												
S	.036	.039	.062	.067	.042	.059	.067	.088	-.032	.083	-.017	-.107
U	.000	.068	.000	.116	.000	.096	.000	.143	.000	.006	.000	-.028
SE	.000	.177	.000	.182	.000	.165	.000	.169	.000	.009	.000	.035
Density												
S	.233[a]	.404[c]	.227[a]	.357[c]	.260[c]	.406[c]	.251[a]	.354[c]	-.124	.146	-.095	.157
U	.001	.005	.001	.005	.001	.005	.001	.004	.000	.289	.000	.000
SE	.001	.001	.001	.001	.000	.001	.001	.001	.000	.252	.000	.000
Per Cent Black												
S	-.085	-.080	-1.038	-.001	-.083	-.074	-1.079	-1.384[a]	-.055	-.067	-.171	.127
U	-.038	-.058	-.464	-.937	-.035	-.051	-.456	-.951	-.003	-.007	-.008	.014
SE	.065	.119	.463	.599	.062	.111	.436	.555	.009	.022	.061	.115
Black/White Median Income												
S	-.220[a]	-.140	-.209[a]	-.206[a]	-.251[a]	-.152	-.243[a]	-.226[a]	.167	.021	.196	.044
U	-12.650	-12.310	-12.039	18.140	13.649	-12.582	-13.214	-18.726	.999	.272	1.175	.586
SE	7.280	9.694	7.607	10.438	6.859	9.031	7.165	9.672	.949	1.821	.998	1.999
Per Cent Poor												
S	-.255[a]	-.145	-.301[a]	-.227	-.263[a]	-.143	-.314[a]	-.236	-.054	-.067	-.040	-.032
U	-.289	-.335	-.342	-.525	-.283	-.312	-.337	-.513	-.006	-.023	-.005	-.011
SE	.145	.356	.165	.382	.137	.332	.155	.354	.019	.067	.022	.073
Per Capita City Revenue												
S	.280[b]	.177[a]	.279[b]	.150	.282[a]	.171[a]	.281[b]	.142	.129	.104	.132	.107
U	.024	.008	.023	.007	.022	.008	.022	.006	.001	.001	.001	.001
SE	.009	.005	.009	.005	.009	.004	.009	.005	.001	.001	.001	.001
Crime Rate												
S	.472[c]	.383[c]	.459[a]	.390[a]	.444[a]	.394[a]	.433[c]	.401[c]	.506[c]	.083	.473[b]	.080
U	.280	.175	.272	.178	.248	.169	.242	.173	.031	.006	.029	.005
SE	.066	.049	.071	.048	.063	.045	.066	.044	.009	.009	.009	.009
(Per Cent Black)²												
S	—	—	2.480	2.375	—	—	2.539	2.560	—	—	.755	-.234
U	—	—	.021	.027	—	—	.021	.028	—	—	.001	.000
SE	—	—	.021	.020	—	—	.020	.019	—	—	.003	.004
(Per Cent Black)³												
S	—	—	-1.580	-1.187	—	—	-1.596	-1.263	—	—	.676	.015
U	—	—	.000	.000	—	—	.000	.000	—	—	.000	.000
SE	—	—	.000	.000	—	—	.000	.000	—	—	.000	.000
R^2	.527[c]	.398[c]	.539[c]	.423[c]	.530[c]	.411	.543[c]	.442[c]	.260[a]	.064	.270	.067

[a] p(for one-tailed test) < .05 [b] p < .01 [c] p < .001

Table A.7
Zero Order Correlation Matrix with Means and Standard Deviations for Total Population and Regional Subpopulations, 1970 and 1980

City Characteristics	1 (1970)	1 (1980)	2 (1970)	2 (1980)	3 (1970)	3 (1980)	4 (1970)	4 (1980)	5 (1970)	5 (1980)	6 (1970)	6 (1980)	7 (1970)	7 (1980)	8 (1970)	8 (1980)	9 (1970)	9 (1980)	10 (1970)	10 (1980)	11 (1970)	11 (1980)	X̄ 1970	X̄ 1980	S.D. 1970	S.D. 1980
1. Total Expenditures for Police																										
(A) All Cities***	—	—	.99c	.98c	.42c	.30c	.43c	.30c	-.09	.01	.53c	.36c	.46c	.19c	.04	.22c	.11	-.05	.62c	.46c	.69c	.44c	25.57	44.49	12.20	18.82
(B) S and W Cities***	—	—	.99c	.99c	.44c	.20c	.35c	.13a	-.10	-.08	.57c	.26c	.41c	.35c	-.11	-.03	.06	-.06	.67c	.51c	.72c	.39c	23.72	42.61	11.92	17.81
(C) N and NC Cities***	—	—	.99c	.98c	.43c	.38c	.58c	.52c	-.22b	.34c	.54c	.41c	.54c	.13	.46c	.50c	.08	-.08	.64c	.47c	.65c	.46c	27.84	46.63	12.19	19.72
2. Salaries and Operations																										
A			—	—	.34c	.12a	.41c	.30c	-.09	.01	.54c	.38c	.44c	.19c	.02	.22c	.13	-.07a	.62c	.45c	.69c	.45c	24.65	42.52	11.79	18.11
B			—	—	.34c	.03	.33c	.13a	-.10	-.08	.57c	.26c	.40c	.36c	-.12	-.03	.08	-.07	.66c	.52c	.72c	.40c	22.75	40.61	11.49	17.47
C			—	—	.34c	.20c	.57c	.53c	-.23b	.35	.55c	.45c	.53c	.13	.45c	.51c	.08	-.11	.65c	.47c	.64c	.48c	27.00	44.69	11.77	18.61
3. Capital Expenditures																										
A					—	—	.29c	.05	-.00	.02	.12	-.02	.31c	.02	.17	.06	-.11	.08	.31c	.11b	.30	.05	.91	1.97	1.09	3.36
B					—	—	.27b	.00	-.04	-.01	.21a	.04	.28c	.03	.10	.00	-.11	.04	.35c	.04	.37c	.03	.97	2.00	1.10	2.93
C					—	—	.32c	.09	-.00	.06	.14	-.05	.39c	.02	.27b	.10	-.08	.13	.25b	.18b	.29c	.06	.84	1.93	1.08	3.79
4. Per Cent Black																										
A							—	—	-.23b	-.17c	.12	.11b	.18a	.10a	.60c	.26c	-.21a	-.28c	.48c	.43c	.25b	.16c	13.70	15.21	13.7	16.78
B							—	—	-.42c	-.38c	.09	.16b	.22b	.06	.60c	.13a	-.40c	-.38c	.28c	.30c	.44c	.27c	14.60	16.75	14.0	17.07
C							—	—	-.20a	.19c	.22b	.35c	.21a	.14b	.65c	.31c	.14	-.11	.71c	.56c	.11a	.10	12.60	13.46	13.3	16.29
5. Per Cent Hispanic																										
A									—	—	-.07	.27c	.03	.08a	.21	.26c	.09	.20c	.25c	.07	-.18a	-.14c	6.89	8.17	9.67	13.28
B									—	—	.09	.38c	.04	.08	.09	.13a	.27b	.42c	.11	-.07	-.18a	-.25c	10.15	11.85	11.69	16.15
C									—	—	-.18a	.57c	.17a	.16b	.19a	.31c	.07	-.09b	.40c	.21c	.19a	.18b	2.87	3.99	3.39	6.96
6. Density																										
A											—	—	.35c	.26c	.08	.16c	.32c	.12b	.25c	.06	.45c	.20c	4.91	4.24	4.36	3.47
B											—	—	.29c	.13a	.06	.10	.19c	.09c	.50c	.05	.50c	.05	3.50	3.48	2.32	2.32
C											—	—	.36c	.31c	.17a	.39c	.27c	-.06	.26b	.15b	.38c	.22c	6.64	5.11	5.53	4.26
7. Population Size																										
A													—	—	.08	.08	-.00	-.08	.24b	.11b	.35c	.32c	192.50	127.35	532.93	363.06
B													—	—	.06	.08	-.03	-.08	.36c	.14	.34c	.22c	161.46	124.19	263.72	215.88
C													—	—	.17a	.17b	-.10	-.10	.38c	.12	.37c	.37c	230.74	130.94	740.28	478.65
8. Per Cent Poor																										
A															—	—	-.39c	-.25c	.26b	.44b	.01	.18c	9.85	10.30	4.51	5.33
B															—	—	-.46c	-.21c	.00	.27c	.04	.14c	11.21	10.91	4.81	5.24
C															—	—	-.04	-.28c	.61c	.60c	.22b	.26c	8.18	9.62	3.46	5.36
9. Black/White Median Income																										
A																	—	—	.07	-.24c	.14	-.09	.68	.72	.15	.21
B																	—	—	.02	-.21c	.02	-.22c	.64	.68	.16	.16
C																	—	—	.10	-.22c	.13	-.05	.72	.76	.12	.20
10. Crime Rate																										
A																			—	—	.38c	.23c	34.30	79.63	14.72	26.23
B																			—	—	.48c	.29c	35.73	84.75	13.72	25.14
C																			—	—	.38c	.29c	32.53	73.82	15.74	26.27
11. Per Capita City Revenue																										
A																					—	—	186.08	520.97	122.10	290.77
B																					—	—	156.09	472.10	106.24	245.82
C																					—	—	223.05	576.49	130.35	326.72

*(A) 1970 N=317   1980 N=566
**(B) 1970 N=175   1980 N=301
***(C) 1970 N=142   1980 N=265

[a] $p < .05$ [b] $p < .01$ [c] $p < .001$

Table A.8
Impact of Percent Hispanic and Other City Characteristics on Policing Expenditures in Cities ≥ 25,000 Population: Regression Results

	Total Expenditures for Police				Salaries and Operations				Capital Expenditures			
	Linear Model		Nonlinear Model		Linear Model		Nonlinear Model		Linear Model		Nonlinear Model	
	1970	1980	1970	1980	1970	1980	1970	1980	1970	1980	1970	1980
Constant	13.295	3.459	12.681	3.513	12.604	3.286	11.852	4.776	.691	.724	.829	-.785
Population Size												
S	.136[c]	-.022	.133[c]	-.038	.122[c]	-.026	.118[c]	-.041	.203[c]	.026	.211[c]	.018
U	.000	-.001	.000	-.002	.000	-.001	.000	-.002	.000	.000	.000	.000
SE	.000	.002	.000	.002	.000	.002	.000	.002	.000	.000	.000	.000
Density												
S	.205[c]	.285[c]	.204[c]	.264[c]	.217[c]	.307[c]	.215	.288[c]	-.049	-.093[a]	-.045	-.104[a]
U	.001	.002	.001	.001	.001	.002	.001	.002	.000	.000	.000	.000
SE	.000	.000	.000	.000	.000	.000	.000	.000	.000	.000	.000	.000
Per Cent Hispanic												
S	.095[b]	.010	.275[a]	.638[c]	.091[b]	.012	.334[a]	.607[a]	.072	.003	-.533[a]	.238
U	.119	.014	.348	.904	.111	.016	.407	.827	.008	.008	-.060	.056
SE	.046	.057	.180	.209	.045	.055	.176	.199	.007	.012	.027	.046
Per Cent Poor												
S	-.273[c]	-.174[c]	-.269[c]	-.098	-.279[c]	-.187[c]	-.274[c]	-.117[a]	-.049	.036	-.051	.074
U	-.741	-.614	-.727	-.348	-.729	-.636	-.715	-.397	-.011	.021	-.012	.043
SE	.121	.184	.126	.190	.119	.175	.124	.180	.019	.039	.019	.041
Per Capita City Revenue												
S	.390[c]	.309[c]	.393[c]	.311[c]	.386[c]	.316[c]	.390[c]	.318[c]	.190[b]	.049	.183[b]	.052
U	.039	.020	.039	.020	.037	.020	.037	.020	.002	.000	.002	.001
SE	.004	.002	.004	.002	.004	.002	.004	.002	.001	.000	.001	.000
Crime Rate												
S	.316[c]	.375[c]	.309[c]	.326[c]	.316[c]	.367[c]	.307[c]	.321[c]	.125[a]	.098[a]	.142[a]	.075
U	.261	.269	.255	.234	.252	.253	.345	.222	.009	.011	.011	.008
SE	.031	.027	.032	.027	.030	.026	.031	.026	.005	.005	.048	.006
Per Cent Black												
S	.297[c]	.197[c]	.301[c]	.175[c]	.291[c]	.203[c]	.297[c]	.183[c]	.178[a]	.031	.161[a]	.020
U	.264	.221	.267	.197	.250	.219	.255	.198	.014	.006	.013	.004
SE	.042	.058	.042	.057	.041	.055	.041	.054	.006	.012	.006	.012
Black/White Median Income												
S	-.082[a]	.042	-.081[a]	.060[a]	-.074[a]	.019	-.073[a]	.035	-.114[a]	.127[c]	-.115[a]	.138[c]
U	-6.682	3.725	-6.574	5.229	-5.852	1.615	-5.735	2.939	-.830	1.849	-.839	2.014
SE	2.857	3.086	2.868	3.063	2.806	2.931	2.810	2.916	.441	.661	.438	.670
(Per Cent Hispanic)[2]												
S	—	—	-.438	-.638[c]	—	—	-.600	-1.161[c]	—	—	1.580[b]	-.366
U	—	—	-.012	.904	—	—	-.016	.025	—	—	.004	-.001
SE	—	—	.010	.209	—	—	.009	.008	—	—	.001	.002
(Per Cent Hispanic)[3]												
S	—	—	.277	.586[c]	—	—	.385	.568[b]	—	—	-1.061[b]	.116
U	—	—	.000	.000	—	—	.198	.000	—	—	.000	.000
SE	—	—	.010	.000	—	—	.121	.000	—	—	.001	.000
R^2	.735[c]	.426[c]	.737[c]	.450[c]	.772[c]	.440[c]	.729[c]	.462[c]	.208[c]	.031[a]	.227[c]	.038[a]

[a] p (for one-tailed test) < .05 [b] p < .01 [c] p < .001

136

Table A.9

Impact of Percent Hispanic and Other City Characteristics on Policing Expenditures in Southern and Western Cities: Regression Results

	Total Expenditures for Police — Linear Model		Nonlinear Model		Salaries and Operations — Linear Model		Nonlinear Model		Capital Expenditures — Linear Model		Nonlinear Model	
	1970	1980	1970	1980	1970	1980	1970	1980	1970	1980	1970	1980
Constant	12.036	5.162	10.887	1.220	11.533	4.331	10.145	.684	.503	1.098	.742	.923
Population Size												
S	.075	.232[c]	.074	.215[c]	.067	.232[c]	.066	.216[c]	.111	.035	.113	.030
U	.001	.019	.000	.018	.000	.019	.000	.017	.000	.000	.000	.000
SE	.000	.004	.000	.004	.000	.004	.000	.004	.000	.001	.000	.001
Density												
S	.122[a]	.185[c]	.123[a]	.167[c]	.127[a]	.182[c]	.130[a]	.166[c]	-.008	-.082	-.015	-.090
U	.001	.001	.001	.001	.001	.001	.001	.001	.000	.000	.000	.000
SE	.000	.000	.000	.000	.000	.000	.000	.000	.000	.000	.000	.000
Percent Hispanic												
S	.109[a]	-.018	.443	.688[c]	.106[a]	-.009	.545[a]	.675[c]	.082	.027	-.891[b]	.090
U	.112	-.020	.452	.759	.104	-.010	.535	.730	.008	.004	-.084	.013
SE	.059	.071	.239	.253	.058	.069	.234	.247	.009	.013	.036	.047
Percent Poor												
S	-.298[c]	-.271[c]	-.290[c]	-.187[b]	-.305[c]	-.281[c]	-.296[c]	-.202[b]	-.051	-.029	-.053	.002
U	-.739	-.920	-.719	-.634	-.727	-.935	-.707	-.672	-.012	-.013	-.012	.001
SE	.169	.251	.180	.269	.166	.244	.177	.263	.026	.046	.027	.050
Per Capita City Revenue												
S	.414[c]	.216[c]	.414[c]	.232[c]	.409[c]	.218[c]	.409[c]	.233[c]	.212[b]	.078	.217[b]	.085
U	.046	.016	.046	.017	.044	.016	.044	.017	.002	.001	.002	.001
SE	.006	.003	.006	.003	.006	.003	.006	.003	.001	.001	.001	.001
Crime Rate												
S	.321[c]	.450[c]	.310[c]	.419[c]	.315[c]	.453[c]	.301[c]	.423[c]	.191[b]	.045	.219[b]	.037
U	.278	.319	.269	.296	.264	.314	.252	.294	.015	.004	.017	.004
SE	.046	.033	.046	.033	.045	.032	.046	.032	.007	.006	.007	.006
Percent Black												
S	.238[b]	.159[a]	.260[c]	.151[a]	.236[b]	.166[a]	.265[c]	.159[a]	.117	.041	.047	.029
U	.202	.166	.220	.157	.193	.170	.217	.163	.009	.006	.363	.004
SE	.006	.082	.067	.081	.065	.080	.066	.079	.010	.015	1.002	.015
Black/White Median Income												
S	-.085	.059	-.087	.056	-.076	.049	-.079	.046	-.128	.052	-.119	.060
U	-6.384	4.787	-6.543	4.592	-5.502	3.940	-5.724	3.686	-.883	.567	-.820	.655
SE	3.884	4.099	3.890	4.099	3.823	3.999	3.811	4.003	.589	.754	.580	.767
(Percent Hispanic)²												
S	—	—	-.799	-1.468[c]	—	—	-1.1064[a]	-1.438[c]	—	—	2.459[b]	.018
U			-.017	-.024			-.022	-.023			.005	.000
SE			.011	.009			.001	.008			.002	.002
(Percent Hispanic)³												
S	—	—	.505	.787[b]	—	—	.679[a]	.782[b]	—	—	-1.626[b]	-.104
U			.000	.000			.000	.000			.000	.000
SE			.000	.000			.000	.000			.000	.000
R²	.712[c]	.472[c]	.715[c]	.491[c]	.698[c]	.478[c]	.705[c]	.495[c]	.213[c]	.014	.249[c]	.016

[a] p (for one-tailed test) < .05
[b] p < .01
[c] p < .001

137

Table A.10
Impact of Percent Hispanic and Other City Characteristics on Policing Expenditures in Northern and North Central Cities: Regression Results

| | Total Expenditures for Police | | | | Salaries and Operations | | | | Capital Expenditures | | | |
| | Linear Model | | Nonlinear Model | | Linear Model | | Nonlinear Model | | Linear Model | | Nonlinear Model | |
	1970	1980	1970	1980	1970	1980	1970	1980	1970	1980	1970	1980
Constant	16.728	14.696	15.741	13.514	15.797	17.374	14.930	13.514	.930	-1.971	.811	-2.383
Population Size												
S	.192c	.151c	.201c	.167c	.172c	.167c	.180c	.167c	.290c	.044	.301c	.036
U	.000	-.006	.000	-.007	.000	-.006	.000	-.007	.000	.000	.000	.000
SE	.000	.002	.000	.002	.000	.002	.001	.002	.000	.001	.000	.000
Density												
S	.244c	.186	.244c	.225c	.258c	.230	.258c	.225c	-.059	-.164a	-.060	-.163a
U	.001	.001	.001	.001	.001	.001	.001	.001	.000	.000	.000	.000
SE	.000	.000	.000	.000	.000	.000	.000	.000	.000	.000	.000	.000
Per Cent Hispanic												
S	-.021	.095a	.125	.230	-.010	.080	.124	.230	-.134a	.103	.063	.521a
U	-.076	.269	.452	.651	-.033	.214	.431	.651	-.043	.056	.020	.284
SE	.151	.160	.767	.563	.150	.146	.761	.563	.025	.042	.125	.149
Per Cent Poor												
S	-.084	-.011	-.074	-.008	-.094	-.024	-.084	-.008	.069	.090	.083	.110
U	-.297	-.041	-.260	-.031	-.319	-.083	-.286	-.031	.022	.063	.026	.077
SE	.204	.266	.210	.268	.203	.242	.209	.268	.033	.069	.034	.070
Per Capita City Revenue												
S	.409c	.386c	.407c	.367c	.402c	.098c	.400c	.367c	.244b	-.006	.241b	-.024
U	.038	.023	.038	.022	.036	.023	.036	.022	.002	.000	.002	.000
SE	.005	.003	.005	.003	.005	.003	.005	.003	.001	.000	.001	.000
Crime Rate												
S	.171b	.147	.167b	.147b	.190b	.118a	.187b	.147b	-.141	.127	-.147	.113
U	.133	.111	.129	.111	.142	.084	.139	.111	-.010	.016	-.010	.014
SE	.050	.045	.051	.045	.050	.041	.051	.045	.008	.010	.008	.011
Percent Black												
S	.388c	.299c	.381c	.309c	.371c	.363c	.365c	.309c	.336b	.004	.327b	-.031
U	.355	.432	.349	.374	.328	.414	.322	.374	.027	.001	.027	-.007
SE	.061	.098	.062	.083	.061	.074	.062	.083	.010	.021	.010	.022
Black/White Median Income												
S	-.109b	.006	-.105b	.013	-.104a	-.032	-.100a	.013	-.100	.183c	-.094	.195c
U	-10.877	.630	-10.441	1.267	-9.992	-2.897	-9.610	1.267	-.885	3.408	-.830	3.644
SE	4.390	4.517	4.500	4.522	4.355	4.113	4.468	4.521	.712	1.189	.730	1.194
(Percent Hispanic)2												
S	—	—	-.458	-.066	—	—	-.419	-.066	—	—	-.009	-.871
U			-.082	-.004			-.072	-.004			.010	-.010
SE			.099	.030			.099	.030			.016	.008
(Percent Hispanic)3												
S	—	—	.343	-.114	—	—	.314	-.114	—	—	.453	.478
U			.022	.000			.002	.000			.000	.000
SE			.003	.000			.003	.000			.000	.000
R²	.783c	.508c	.784c	.517c	.770c	.541c	.772c	.517c	.274c	.066a	.276c	.078a

a p (for one-tailed test) <.05
b p<.01
c p<.001

References

Albuquerque Journal. 2/9/72. "Commission Seeks Probe."
_____. 2/20/72. "Plea For Probe in Beret Deaths Claimed Rejected."
_____. 3/9/72. "'Justifiable Homicide' Ruled in Beret Deaths."
_____. 3/11/72. "Berets, Lawyers Say Jury Broke Secrecy."
_____. 5/25/72. "Police Chief Asks $2.9 Million More."
_____. 7/10/72. "Police Brutality is Alleged Before Rights Committee."
_____. 8/12/72. "Seven Anti-Property Crime Projects Approved by COG."
_____. 5/1/79. "FBI Probing Alleged APD Rights Violations."
_____. 2/26/80. "Fund Shortage May End APD 'Sting' Operations."
Atlanta Journal. 1/18/73. "Atlanta's First Black Officer's Honored."
_____. 3/27/73. "Jackson Calls Probe 'Racial.'"
_____. 7/19/73. "Police Can Meet Rights Deadline."
_____. 12/7/73. "Arrested Girl's Mom Sues Atlanta Police."
_____. 1/18/79. "Jackson Likely to Fight for Police, Firemen's Pay."
_____. 3/29/79. "Atlanta Police, Firemen Rank at Bottom in Pay."
_____. 4/10/79. "Houston Recruiting Police Officers in City."
_____. 4/11/79. "Mayor Vows to Seek More Pay for Police."
_____. 4/24/79. "Mayor Links Police Raises to Tax Boost."
_____. 6/27/79. "50–50 Police Promotion Quota Puts Mayor on the Firing Line."
_____. 11/11/79. "Plan Would Shift City's Police Reins."
_____. 11/12/79. "Police, Firemen to Get Pay Hikes."
_____. 11/13/79. "Blacks Assail Takeover Plan as Racist Ploy."
_____. 11/15/79. "Busbee Against Shifting Police."
_____. 1/9/80. "City Police Threaten a Sick-Out Over Pay."
_____. 1/25/80. "Witnesses Urge Council to Hike Police Salaries."
_____. 1/28/80. "Brown Defends Request for 600 More Policemen."
_____. 2/2/80. "Mayor Reverses Himself, Again Asks for 200 More Police."
_____. 2/8/80. "City Police Demand Talks, Threaten Job Action."

_____. 3/30/80. "22 Recruits Added to Police Force Here."

_____. 5/16/80. "5-Year Plan Reshapes Police."

_____. 11/10/80. "Jammed Police Academy Sidetracks Recruits from Duty."

Becker, Gary. 1968. "Crime and Punishment: An Economic Approach." *Journal of Political Economy,* March/April: 169-217.

Becker, Howard. 1963. *Outsiders: Studies in the Sociology of Deviance.* New York: Macmillan.

Blalock, Hubert. 1967. *Toward a Theory of Minority Group Relations.* New York: John Wiley.

Blau, Judith R., and Peter M. Blau. 1982. "Metropolitan Structure and Violent Crime." *American Sociological Review* 47: 114-128.

Boggs, Sarah L. 1965. "Urban Crime Patterns." *American Sociological Review* 30: 899-905.

Bohannan, Paul. 1973. "The Differing Realms of Law." Pp. 306-317 in D. Black and M. Mileski, eds. *The Social Organization of Law.* New York: Seminar Press.

Brantingham, Paul, and Patricia Brantingham. 1984. *Patterns in Crime.* New York: Macmillan.

Brazer, Harvey E. 1959. *City Expenditures in the United States.* New York: National Bureau of Economic Research (Occasional paper #66).

Button, James W. 1978. *Black Violence: Political Impact of the 1960s Riots.* Princeton, NJ: Princeton University Press.

Carroll, Leo, and Pamela Irving Jackson. 1983. "Inequality, Opportunity, and Crime Rates in Central Cities." *Criminology* 21 (2): 178-194.

Chicago Courier. 9/22/72. "Kenner Asks Probe."

Chicago Daily News. 6/12/72. "Charges 'Vague'—Hanrahan."

_____. 6/26/72. "Daley: 'I Won't Fire Conlisk.'"

_____. 7/11/72. "Hanrahan 'Negligent' in Raid Probe—Sears."

_____. 7/24/72. "CCHR Pinpoints Cop Abuse Causes."

Chicago Sun-Times. 3/31/72. "Jury to Get 25 Charges of Police Brutality."

_____. 5/16/72. "High Court Rejects Plan of Hanrahan on Panthers."

_____. 5/18/72. "Order Quiz on Police Brutality."

_____. 5/31/72. "Sears Limits Evidence on Hanrahan."

_____. 6/27/72. "Daley Won't Fire Conlisk; Backs Him 100%."

_____. 9/1/72. "U.S. Freeze on Aid to Chicago Police Urged by Robinson."

_____. 9/6/72. "Find Unintentional Job Bias Here."

_____. 12/4/72. "Community Control of the Police."

_____. 12/7/72. "City Bar Urges Unit As Police Monitors."

_____. 12/8/72. "Bar's Proposal to Review Police Brutality Cases Scored."

_____. 12/23/72. "Conlisk Sued on 'Police Brutality.'"

_____. 2/14/79. "Probe Strip-Search of Women by Police."

_____. 2/16/79. "State Repeals Its Strip-Search Recommendations."

_____. 8/11/79. "DiLeonardi to Shuffle 30 Top Cops, Promote Mob Foes."

_____. 8/15/79. "58 Cops Shifted to Street Patrols."

_____. 8/16/79. "Cop Shake-Up Widens; 45 Shifted."

_____. 10/13/79. "Police Beef-Up, Shuffle Promised."

_____. 10/22/79. "Police Understaffed to Save Cash."

_____. 9/28/80. "Guns Link Two Cops to Mob Killings."

_____. 9/29/80. "Mob Chief Linked to Cop 'Gun Plot.'"

Chicago Tribune. 4/25/72. "Metcalf Demands Police Change Ways With Blacks."
_____. 4/29/72. "Black Dentist, Held As Drunk, Dies of Stroke."
_____. 5/5/72. "Police Groups Hit Civilian Review Plan."
_____. 5/6/72. "Black Demands Conlisk's Ouster; 2nd Hits the System."
_____. 5/13/72. "Won't Change Police System, Conlisk Insists."
_____. 5/16/72. "U.S. Supreme Court Refuses to Hear Hanrahan's Appeal in Panther Case."
_____. 5/18/72. "Conlisk Orders Police to Stop Harassing Latins."
_____. 5/31/72. "Police Unit Head Raps Civilian Role."
_____. 7/6/72. "New Charges Made in Panthers Case."
_____. 7/11/72. "Hanrahan, Others Waive Jury Trial in Panther Case."
_____. 4/21/79. "Levi to Head Police Board."
_____. 4/24/79. "New Panther Trial Ordered."
_____. 7/24/79. "Stanley Approved for Police Board."
_____. 8/16/79. "DiLeonardi Shifts 41 Officers in Top Level Shake-Up of Police."
_____. 8/28/79. "Police Motor Pool Scandal."
_____. 8/29/79. "Cop Scandal Probe Grows."
_____. 8/31/79. "$3.5 Million Overcharges for Repairs on Police Cars."
_____. 10/10/79. "Murphy Won't Seek Police Chief Post."
_____. 10/13/79. "Byrne Wavers on DiLeonardi As Chief of Police; Leans Toward A Top Aide."
_____. 1/12/80. "Brzeczek Appointed As Top Cop."
_____. 9/24/80. "Byrne Names Committee to Probe Police Brutality."
Cohen, Lawrence E., and Marcus Felson. 1979. "Social Change and Crime Rate Trends." *American Sociological Review* 44: 588-607.
Community Relations Service. 1973, 1974. *Annual Report of the Community Relations Service*. Washington, DC: U.S. Government Printing Office.
Daily Defender. 1/24/72. "Poor Mr. S; He Ran Afoul of the Law."
_____. 4/1/72. "The Black Watch."
_____. 4/25/72. "Conlisk Considers 6 Demands."
_____. 7/11/72a. "Bench Trial for Hanrahan."
_____. 7/11/72b. "Attack Probe Chief: Renault: Cop Bias Quiz a Fraud."
_____. 12/7/72. "Metcalf Attacks Police Plan."
_____. 6/12/80. "Black Southside Family Charges Police Brutality."
_____. 9/24/80. "New Commission to Probe Police Brutality Charges."
_____. 9/29/80. "Community Speaks Out On Police Brutality."
Denver Post. 1/14/72. "Mayor Pledges Crime Fight."
_____. 1/16/72. "Denver Aid From LEAA Due Soon."
_____. 1/27/72. "Relations Report Studied."
_____. 2/23/72. "72 Will Help Slice Anti Crime Funds Pie."
_____. 2/27/72. "Lewis Says Case Open on Young."
_____. 3/5/72. "Young's Lawyers Reject 'No Blood' Explanation."
_____. 4/24/72. "Bullets in Young Body Yield No Conclusions."
_____. 5/8/72. "Arthur Dill Named as Police Chief."
_____. 7/31/72. "Police Chicago Harassment Charged."
_____. 8/1/72. "Civil Rights Complaints Allege Police Brutality."
_____. 8/7/72. "Seven Blacks Seek Police Jobs."
_____. 8/17/72. "Threat of Sanctions Made."

———. 8/23/72. "Unit Seeks Minority Firemen, Policemen."

Detroit Free Press. 8/29/72. "White Policemen Face Discipline Over Beatings."

———. 10/29/72. "Police Dept Facing Racial Crisis."

———. 11/6/72. "Black Gain Found in City Police."

———. 1/22/79. "Black Civilian Woman Leads Detroit Police Policy Makers."

———. 6/24/79. "Programs, Not Police, Called Curb for Crime."

———. 11/25/79. "Detroit Police: The Long March From 1976."

———. 5/9/80. "Council Asks Crackdown on Police Misconduct."

———. 8/3/80. "Police Brutality, Misconduct Cases Cost Millions."

———. 8/10/80. "How Tough Precinct Was Turned Around."

———. 8/11/80. "Cops: Are They the Good Guys?"

———. 8/31/80. "Six Years After Its Inception, Review Board Fulfills Its Mandate."

———. 11/10/80. "Police Doing Well In Spite of Layoffs."

———. 12/7/80. "City Police: A Past of Racism, Brutality."

Diamond, Stanley. 1973. "The Rule of Law versus the Order of Custom." Pp. 318-314 in Donald Black and Maureen Mileski, eds., *The Social Organization of Law.* New York: Seminar Press.

Evans, Arthur S., and M. W. Giles. 1986. "Effects of Percent Black and Blacks' Perceptions of Relative Power and Social Distance." *Journal of Black Studies* 17: 3-14.

Evening Bulletin (Philadelphia). 2/26/79. "Commission Sets Brutality Hearings."

———. 8/13/79. "U.S. Suit Charges Brutality."

———. 8/14/79. "Mayor is Eager to Battle Charges."

———. 8/20/79. "Cops Ready for 'War.'"

———. 9/5/79. "Philadelphia Moves to Kill U.S. Police Abuse Suit."

———. 10/31/79. "Police Suit 'Carefully Cultivated' Judge Says."

———. 12/14/79. "Last of Brutality Suit Dismissed."

———. 1/17/80. "Solomon Studies Brutality Issue."

———. 2/16/80. "Police Size Has No Effect on Crime Rate, Report Says."

———. 2/26/80. "U.S. Pushes Brutality Suit Against Cops."

———. 3/18/80. "Report Forsees Phila. Needing Fewer Police."

———. 7/2/80. "Phila. Policeman Fired Over Deadly-Force Rules."

———. 8/26/80. "Crowd Stones Police Station."

———. 8/31/80. "The Cop Didn't Have to Kill That Brother."

———. 9/2/80. "Under Commissioner, Police 'Walk the Line.'"

———. 10/9/80. "'Deadly Force' Rule is Tougher in Other Cities, Study Finds."

Feagin, Joseph R., and Harlan Hahn. 1973. *Ghetto Revolts: The Politics of Violence in American Cities.* New York: Macmillan.

Federal Bureau of Investigation. 1974. *Annual Report of the Federal Bureau of Investigation.* Washington, DC: U.S. Government Printing Office.

Feeley, Malcolm M., and Austin D. Sarat. 1980. *The Policy Dilemma.* Minneapolis: University of Minnesota Press.

Fischer, Claude S. 1984. *The Urban Experience,* 2nd ed. San Diego: Harcourt Brace Jovanovich.

Florida-Times-Union. 4/27/80. "Shoot-To-Kill Law Limitations Recommended."

Garofalo, James. 1979. "Victimization and the Fear of Crime." *Journal of Research in Crime and Delinquency* 16: 80-97.

Gastil, R. D. 1971. "Homicide and a Regional Culture of Violence." *American*

Sociological Review 36: 412-417.

Giles, M. W. 1977. "Recent Black and Racial Hostility: An Old Assumption Re-examined." *Social Science Quarterly* 58: 412-417.

Goodman, Robert. 1979. *The Last Entrepreneurs: America's Regional Wars for Jobs and Dollars.* New York: Simon and Schuster.

Gove, Walter. 1975. *The Labeling of Deviance: Evaluating a Perspective.* New York: John Wiley.

Greenberg, David F. 1979. *Mathematical Criminology.* New Brunswick, NJ: Rutgers University Press.

Greenberg, David F., Ronald C. Kessler, and Colin Loftin. 1983. "The Effect of Police Employment on Crime." *Criminology* 21 (3): 375-394.

Greenwood, Michael J., and Walter J. Wadycki. 1973. "Crime Rates and Public Expenditures for Police Protection: Their Interaction." *Review of Social Economy* 31: 138-151.

Hackney, S. 1969. "Southern Violence." *American Historical Review* 74: 906-925.

Harries, Keith D. 1971. "The Geography of American Crime, 1968." *Journal of Geography* 70: 204-213.

_____. 1974. *The Geography of Crime and Justice.* New York: McGraw-Hill.

Heinz, A., H. Jacob, and R. L. Lineberry, eds. 1983. *Crime in City Politics.* New York: Longman.

Huff, C. Ronald, and John M. Stahura. 1980. "Police Employment and Suburban Crime." *Criminology* 17 (4): 461-470.

Jackson, Pamela Irving. 1978. "Community Control, Community Mobilization, and Community Political Structure in 57 U.S. Cities." *The Sociological Quarterly* 19: 577-589.

_____. 1984. "Opportunity and Crime: A Function of City Size." *Sociology and Social Research* 69 (2): 172-193.

_____. 1985. "Ethnicity, Region, and Public Fiscal Commitment to Policing." *Justice Quarterly* 2 (2): 167-194.

_____. 1986. "Black Visibility, City Size, and Social Control." *The Sociological Quarterly* 27 (2): 185-203.

_____. forthcoming. "Minority Group Threat and Social Control: Twenty Years of Investigation." In Michael Dobkowski and Isidor Wallimann, eds. *Research in Inequality and Social Conflict,* Volume II. Greenwich, CT: JAI Press.

Jackson, Pamela Irving, and Leo Carroll. 1981. "Race and the War on Crime: The Sociopolitical Determinants of Municipal Police Expenditures in 90 U.S. Cities." *American Sociological Review* 46: 290-305.

Jacobs, David. 1979. "Inequality and Police Strength: Conflict Theory and Coercive Control in Metropolitan Areas." *American Sociological Review* 44: 913-925.

_____. 1982. "Inequality and Economic Crime." *Sociology and Social Research* 66: 12-28.

Kowalski, G. S., R. L. Dittman, Jr., and W. L. Bung. 1980. "Spatial Distribution of Criminal Offenses by States, 1970-1976." *Journal of Research in Crime and Delinquency* 17: 4-25.

Larson, Richard C. 1972. *Urban Police Patrol Analysis.* Cambridge, MA: MIT Press.

Law Enforcement Assistance Administration. 1971, 1978a. *Expenditures and Employment Data for the Criminal Justice System.* Washington, DC: U.S. Government Printing Office.

_____. 1978b. *Criminal Victimization in the United States.* Washington, DC: U.S. Government Printing Office.

Lemert, Edwin. 1951. *Social Pathology.* New York: McGraw-Hill.

Liska, Allen E. 1987. "A Critical Examination of Macro Perspectives on Crime Control." *Annual Review of Sociology* 13: 67-88.

Liska, Allen E., and William F. Baccaglini. 1983. "Fear of Crime." Pp. 765-768 in *Encyclopedia of Crime and Justice* (2), Sanford H. Kadish, ed. New York: Free Press.

Liska, Allen E., and Mitchell B. Chamlin. 1984. "Social Structure and Crime Control Among Macrosocial Units." *American Journal of Sociology* 90 (2): 383-395.

Liska, Allen E., Mitchell B. Chamlin, and Mark D. Reed. 1985. "Testing the Economic Production and Conflict Models of Crime Control." *Social Forces* 64 (1): 119-138.

Liska, Allen E., Joseph J. Lawrence, and Michael Benson. 1981. "Perspectives on the Legal Order: The Capacity for Social Control." *American Journal of Sociology* 87: 413-426.

Liska, Allen E., Joseph J. Lawrence, and Andrew Sanchirico. 1982. "Fear of Crime as a Social Fact." *Social Forces* 60 (3): 760-770.

Liska, Allen E., and Jiang Yu. 1987. "Specifying and Testing the Conflict Perspective on Crime Control: Police Use of Deadly Force." Paper presented at the Annual Meeting of the American Society of Criminology, Montreal, Quebec, Canada.

Lizotte, Alan J., and David J. Bordua. 1980. "Firearms Ownership for Sport and Protection." *American Sociological Review* 45: 229-243.

Loftin, Colin, and Robert Hill. 1974. "Regional Subculture of Violence: An Examination of the Gastil-Hackney Thesis." *American Sociological Review* 39: 714-724.

Loftin, Colin, and David McDowell. 1982. "The Police, Crime, and Economic Theory: An Assessment." *American Sociological Review* 47: 393-401.

Mansfield, Roger, Leroy C. Gould, and J. Zvi Namenwirth. 1974. "A Socioeconomic Model for the Prediction of Societal Rates of Property Theft." *Social Forces* 52: 462-472.

Mayhew, Bruce H., and Robert L. Levinger. 1976. "Size and the Density of Interaction in Human Aggregates." *American Journal of Sociology* 82: 86-110.

McPheters, Lee R., and William B. Stronge. 1974. "Law Enforcement Expenditures and Urban Crime." *National Tax Journal* 27: 633-644.

Messner, Steven F. 1983. "Regional Differences in the Economic Correlates of the Urban Homicide Rate." *Criminology* 21: 477-488.

Miami Herald. 1/15/72. "Why We're No. 0 in Funds To Fight Crime in Streets."

_____. 11/9/72. "PBA Vote Drops Bar to Blacks."

_____. 12/20/72. "Officer's Firing Upheld in Abuse Case."

_____. 12/28/72. "Damage Suit Filed Against Two Miami Police Officers."

_____. 2/27/79. "Citizens May Review Police."

_____. 4/18/79. "NAACP Asks Federal Probe of Alleged Police Brutalities."

_____. 7/22/79. "Brutal Policemen Keep Badges, Guns."

_____. 7/23/79. "Metro's Meanest? A Look at 9 Officers."

_____. 7/24/79. "15 Officers Expensive for City."

_____. 7/25/79a. "Police Operate in World of Hostility."

_____. 7/25/79b. "Stress of Job Makes Some Turn to Brutality."

_____. 7/26/79a. "Agencies Seek Ways to Police the Police."

_____. 7/26/79b. "Police Discipline Hidden in Secrecy."

_____. 1/4/80. "Among 196 with Many Complaints."

_____. 1/9/80. "Mental Tests for Cops."

_____. 5/20/80. "'Dual Prosecution' Rights Law Used Sparingly."

_____. 6/16/80. "Federal Jurors Tackling Brutality Cases."

_____. 6/28/80. "City Creates Agency to Pursue Police Complaints."

_____. 7/28/80. "Police Put Brutality Reforms Into Effect."

_____. 7/31/80. "McDuffie Cops' Complaint Rate is High."

_____. 8/6/80. "'LaFleur Cops' Complaint Rate is High."

_____. 9/21/80. "Psychologist Would Fire Most of Class."

_____. 12/22/80. "150 Join McDuffie Memorial."

_____. 12/28/80. "Police Justice Not Always Blind to Color."

_____. 12/30/80. "Justice System Reforms Aim at Roots of Police Misconduct."

Miami Times. 10/11/72. "PBA Loses Fight, Must Take Blacks."

_____. 10/19/72. "PBA Loses."

_____. 10/23/72. "Failure to Reach Settlement Means Back to Federal Court."

_____. 12/22/72. "Police-Community Relations To Improve."

Michalowski, Raymond J. 1985. *Order, Law and Crime.* New York: Random House.

Michigan Chronicle. 7/8/72. "Rampant Corruption in Police Dept. Told."

_____. 11/25/72. "UL Report Hails Black Cop Hiring Progress, Asks More."

Miller, Walter. 1958. "Lower Class Culture as a Generating Milieu of Gang Delinquency." *Journal of Social Issues* 14: 5-19.

Minneapolis Tribune. 5/24/72. "Police Chief Says Badges Need Not Be Displayed."

_____. 8/29/72. "Judge Says Police Attacked War Protesters and By-Standers."

_____. 12/27/72. "Stenvig Defends Police Manpower-Use Policy."

_____. 6/12/79. "Audit Reveals Police Pension Financial Woes."

_____. 6/20/79. "Plan to Train Minority Police Announced."

_____. 7/23/79. "Police Politics Already Heavy in Mayor's Race."

_____. 7/29/79a. "City Prostitution Tied to Police Corruption."

_____. 7/29/79b. "Chief Asks Probe of Charges."

_____. 7/31/79a. "County Planning No City Police Probe."

_____. 7/31/79b. "Unsuccessful Tippling House Raid A Part of Current Police Bickering."

_____. 8/4/79a. "Deputy Chief: Political Influences Ruining Police Force."

_____. 8/4/79b. "O'Meara Gives Up on Seeking Reforms."

_____. 8/7/79. "Newsletter Asks Nordlund to Resign."

_____. 8/10/79. "Nordlund Resigns as Police Chief."

_____. 8/19/79. "Police Officer Promoted While Investigated."

_____. 8/26/79. "Candidates Agree: Police, Politics Don't Mix."

_____. 9/5/79. "Johnson Says Police Records Inadequate For Misconduct Probe."

_____. 9/28/79. "Police Watchdog System Criticized."

_____. 7/25/80. "Police Brutality Complaints Fall by Half in Minneapolis This Year."

_____. 10/17/80. "Lindberg Named to Head Police Internal Affairs Unit."

_____. 11/1/80. "Council Wants Police Manpower Minimums."

Newark Evening News. 4/28/72. "FBI Asked to Check Cop Charge."

_____. 5/30/72. "Arrest of Mail Driver Triggers Dual Probe."

_____. 6/2/72. "Mailman, Cop Charges To Be Aired on June 21."

Newsbank. 1972, 1979, and 1980. Urban Affairs Library. Stamford, CT.: Newsbank, Inc.

Oakland Tribune. 11/20/80. "Study Urges Stress Treatment for Police Officers."

Ogburn, W. F. 1935. "Factors in Variation of Crime Among Cities." *Journal of the American Statistical Association* 30: 12-20.

Oklahoma Eagle. 3/16/72. "Subpoena Powers and the CRC."

_____. 9/7/72. "Can CRC Do It?"

_____. 10/12/72. "Expert Says Police Force Needs Blacks."

Philadelphia Inquirer. 4/14/72. "Rizzo Blasts Report Critical of Police."

_____. 5/26/72. "Police Hirings and Promotions Are Not Impartial Judge Says."

_____. 5/29/72. "Why So Few Blacks Color it Blue."

_____. 5/31/72. "City Appeals Decision on Police Race Ratio."

_____. 6/25/72. "Will Cop on Every Corner Plan Really Halt Crime?"

_____. 7/8/72. "Police Hiring of Blacks Set at 1-for-2 Rate."

_____. 9/13/72. "City's High Crime Areas Need More Police, Study Reveals."

_____. 10/5/72. "Rizzo to Hire 1500 More Cops Before 'My First Term Is Up.'"

_____. 11/10/72. "U.S. Court Reinstate 2-1 Hiring Plan."

_____. 8/19/79. "Text of the U.S. Suit Alleging Abuse by Phila. Police . . . ."

_____. 1/13/80. "At the Police Department, A New Broom Sweeps Fast."

_____. 4/20/80. "When Can Police Shoot? New Rules Are Coming."

_____. 10/19/80. "It Is Solomon, More Than Rule, Riling the Police."

Philadelphia Tribune. 5/30/72. "Ask Help of Rizzo to Fill City Quota of Black Policemen."

_____. 7/18/72. "Police Aid Delayed by Hassle."

_____. 8/15/72. "Black Officials Demand Probe of Police Violence."

Porter, Bruce and Marvin Dunn. 1984. *The Miami Riot of 1980: Crossing the Bounds.* Lexington, MA: D.C. Heath and Co.

President's Commission on Law Enforcement and Administration of Justice. 1967. *The Challenge of Crime in a Free Society.* Washington, DC: U.S. Government Printing Office.

Pyle, Gerald F. 1976. "Geographic Perspectives in Crime and the Impact of Anticrime Legislation." Pp. 257-291 in John S. Adams, ed. *Urban Policymaking and Metropolitan Dynamics: A Comparative Geographic Analysis.* Cambridge, MA: Ballinger.

Quinney, Richard. 1970. *The Social Reality of Crime.* Boston, MA: Little, Brown.

Reiss, Albert J., and David J. Bordua. 1967. "Environment and Organization: A Perspective on the Police." Pp. 25-55 in David J. Bordua, ed. *The Police: Six Sociological Essays.* New York: John Wiley.

Reppetto, Thomas. 1974. *Residential Crime.* Cambridge: Ballinger.

Rocky Mountain News. 2/19/79. "Tensions Ease Between Police and Hispanos."

Rubinstein, Johnathan. 1973. *City Police.* New York: Farrar, Straus and Giroux.

Sacramento Bee. 4/8/72. "State Unit Plans to Probe Area Police Job Bias Charge."

_____. 8/10/72. "Witnesses Say Deputies Acted Brutally in Arresting 3 Men."

_____. 12/30/72. "After Indictment and Police Unit Request: Quit Chasing Felons."

_____. 2/2/79. "Dispute Points Told by County."

_____. 3/11/79. "Probation Patrol Effective."

_____. 7/16/80. "Mexican-American Group: Stop Police Harassment."

_____. 12/22/80. "Police: A Less Agonizing Wait in Capital."

St. Petersburg Times. 12/22/80. "McDuffie Family Suit Seeks $25-Million in Damages."

San Francisco Chronicle. 4/29/79. "Report on Minority Police Cadets."

_____. 7/20/72. "Special Grant: S.F. Recruiting 20 Black Cops."

San Francisco Examiner. 1/13/79. "Board Told to OK Bias Suit Solution."

_____. 2/28/79. "A Warning for City in Police Suit."

_____. 3/13/79. "Police Bias Pact; Special Fund a Key Factor."

_____. 3/31/79. "Police Bias Pact Ratified by U.S. Judge."

_____. 5/3/79. "Cops Don't Agree with Feinstein That Pay Offer is 'Generous.'"

_____. 5/20/79. "The Different Shades of Blue."

_____. 6/12/79. "Riot Probe Tall Order for Police Commission."

_____. 6/16/79. "Why Cops Failed at Riot."

_____. 6/22/79. "What Public Thinks of Gain."

_____. 6/29/79. "Police Are Accused of Post-Riot Brutality."

_____. 7/4/79. "A Squeeze Play on Gain."

_____. 7/6/79. "Concessions Gain Won."

_____. 7/7/79. "Police Bias Lawyers Unhappy, Return to Court."

_____. 7/13/79. "Community Relations for Police in Works."

_____. 7/17/79. "U.S. Investigating Police-Gay Incident."

_____. 7/22/79. "What Public Thinks of Gain."

_____. 11/1/79. "City Finds Cops Too Late and Too Few."

Schur, Edwin. 1972. *Labeling Deviant Behavior*. New York: Harper and Row.

Seagle, W. 1946. *The History of Law*. New York: Tudor Publications.

Shaw, Clifford R., and Henry D. McKay. 1972. *Juvenile Delinquency and Urban Areas*, rev. ed. Chicago: University of Chicago Press.

Silver, Alan. 1967. "The Demand for Order in Civil Society: A Review of Some Themes in the History of Urban Crime, Police, and Riot." Pp. 1-24 in David J. Bordua, ed. *The Police: Six Sociological Essays*. New York: John Wiley.

Skogan, Wesley G., and Michael G. Maxfield. 1981. *Coping with Crime: Individual and Neighborhood Reactions*. Beverly Hills, CA: Sage.

Skolnick, Jerome H., and David H. Bayley. 1986. *The New Blue Line: Police Innovation in Six American Cities*. New York: Free Press.

Slovak, Jeffrey S. 1987. "Police Organization and Policing Environment: Case Study of a Disjuncture." *Sociological Focus* 20 (1): 77-94.

Star-Ledger (Newark). 1/10/79. "65 Newark Detectives Back in Blue as Shakeup Hits."

_____. 1/22/79. "Police to Picket on Newark Job."

_____. 2/1/79. "Newark 'Selective' on Crime."

_____. 1/17/80. "Gibson Is 'Pessimistic' as Police Win 7% Hike."

_____. 3/5/80. "Gibson to Recall 30 Cops."

_____. 10/24/80. "Council Overrides Gibson's Veto of a Police Minimum."

Sun (Baltimore). 1/6/72. "Police Major Investigated."

_____. 1/27/72a. "Police Probes of Brutality Charges Leave Complainants Unsatisfied."

_____. 1/27/72b. "One Accused Policeman in Four is Found Guilty."

_____. 3/12/72. "City Police Praise Their Air Force."

_____. 4/15/72. "7 Policemen Ordered to Answer Suit Filed by Couple Alleging Brutality."

_____. 5/20/72. "Pomerleau Wins Praise, 2nd Term from Governor."

_____. 5/29/72. "Pomerleau Says Public Must Help."

————. 11/28/72. "2 Patrolmen Accused of Bias Resign."

————. 12/4/72. "Brutality Charged in Lutherville Arrest."

————. 2/14/79. "City Police Patrols Augmented."

————. 4/13/79. "Police Group Predicts More Resignations, Poor Law Enforcement Following Aid Loss."

————. 5/4/79. "Schaefer Pledges Police Aid."

————. 5/6/79. "Police Unit Calls Pay Deplorable."

————. 1/17/80. "Hughes Failure To Deliver Police Aid Angers Schaefer."

————. 2/2/80. "Mayor Lauds Governor For Increasing Aid to City Police."

————. 11/26/80. "Pomerleau Calls Women 'Balls of Fluff' in Bias Case."

Sun Reporter (San Francisco). 9/9/72. "Police Sweeps Enrage Community."

————. 1/4/79. "Black Cops Reject Feinstein's Plan to Settle SFPD Bias Suit."

————. 3/1/79. "Black Female Police Officers Enjoy Their Work."

————. 6/21/79. "Blacks Lost Faith in Chief Gain a Long Time Ago."

————. 7/3/80. "Decision Delayed on Police Detail."

————. 7/17/80. "Battle Starts Over Police-Community Relations."

Tallahassee Democrat. 5/21/80. "McDuffie Verdict Condemned at FAMU Rally."

Time. 1981. "Anger in the Streets." July 20: 30-32.

Tulsa Daily World. 9/4/72. "Black-White Panel Demand Due in Police Probe Here."

————. 9/9/72. "Change in Demeanor of Police Promised."

Turk, Austin T. 1969. *Criminality and the Legal Order.* Chicago: Rand McNally.

U.S. Census. 1970, 1980. *Characteristics of the Population.* Washington, DC: U.S. Government Printing Office.

————. *State and Metropolitan Area Data Book, 1979: A Statistical Abstract Supplement.* Washington, DC: U.S. Government Printing Office.

Wallimann, Isidor. 1984. "The Import of Foreign Workers in Switzerland: Labor-Power Reproduction Costs, Ethnic Antagonism and the Integration of Foreign Workers into Swiss Society." Pp. 153-175 in Louis Kriesberg, ed. *Research in Social Movements, Conflict and Change,* Vol. 7. Greenwich, CT: JAI Press.

Washington Post. 2/16/79. "Chicago Suit Hits Strip Searches of Women by Police."

————. 8/14/79. "Philadelphia Police: Toughest in the World."

Weicher, John C. 1970. "Determinants of Central City Expenditures: Some Overlooked Factors and Problems." *National Tax Journal* 23 (4): 379-396.

Wichita Eagle. 2/11/72. "Coalition Planners O.K. Police Board."

————. 2/18/72. "Police-Community Board Gets HRDAB Endorsement."

————. 2/23/72. "Vote for Crime Board Fires Drive to Oust Porter."

————. 1/6/79. "Task Force Demands Feds Probe Charges Police Brutalized Blacks."

————. 1/18/79a. "Officer Is Reprimanded for 'Rough' Body Search."

————. 1/18/79b. "Miller, Cop at Odds on Racial Fray."

————. 1/19/79. "Stephen May Look Into Brutality Case."

————. 2/16/79. "Public Airs Gripes About Law Officers."

————. 2/17/79. "Chief Defends Police Acts at Race Hearing."

————. 2/23/79. "No Violations Found in Federal Racial Probe."

————. 3/27/79. "Candidates Oppose Civilian Police Review Board."

————. 4/17/79. "Cops Get Riot Training Though Less Than They Did in the 60's."

————. 4/19/79. "Wichita Group to Demand Probe of Police Conduct at Herman Hill."

————. 5/2/79. "Boards to Help Study Complaints on Police."

————. 5/18/79. "Chief: Alternative Study O.K."

_____. 6/24/79. "Part 1—An Overview: How Much of A Problem."

_____. 6/25/79. "Black Perspective: A Picture of Distrust, Fear, Resentment."

_____. 6/27/79. "Police: Duty Calls, But So Does Reality."

_____. 6/28/79. "—Redress: Possible, But Difficult, Citizens Feel."

_____. 8/14/79. "Draft Report on Police Irks Chief."

_____. 10/12/79. "NAACP Sues Wichita over Civil Rights."

_____. 1/15/80. "Police to Limit Arms Use."

_____. 5/13/80. "Federal Rights Study Criticizes Wichita Police, Sheriff's Force."

Wilson, James Q. 1968. *Varieties of Police Behavior*. Cambridge, MA: Harvard University Press.

Wilson, O. W. 1941. *Distribution of Police Patrol Force*. Publication 74. Chicago: Public Administration Service.

_____. 1972. *Police Administration*, 3d ed. New York; McGraw-Hill.

Wilson, William Julius. 1987. *The Truly Disadvantaged: The Inner City, the Underclass, and Public Policy*. Chicago: University of Chicago Press.

Wirth, Louis. 1938. "Urbanism as a Way of Life." *American Journal of Sociology* 44: 1-24.

Wolfgang, Marvin E. 1968. "Urban Crime." Pp. 270-311 in J.Q. Wilson, ed. *The Metropolitan Enigma*. Cambridge, MA: Harvard University Press.

Zelinsky, Wilbur. 1973. *The Cultural Geography of the United States*. Englewood Cliffs, NJ: Prentice-Hall.

Index

ABOUT THE AUTHOR

PAMELA IRVING JACKSON is professor and chair of the Sociology Department and director of the Justice Studies Program at Rhode Island College. She holds a Ph.D. from Brown University and serves as associate editor of the *American Sociological Review.* Articles in *Justice Quarterly, Sociological Quarterly, Criminology,* and the *American Sociological Review* describe her efforts, alone and with others, to develop and extend theoretical understandings and empirical research linking stratification, race relations, and inequality to the nature and level of publicly sponsored social control efforts.

Dr. Jackson regularly teaches courses in crime and criminal justice, as well as data analysis, and is active in major professional organizations, making recent presentations at meetings of the American Society of Criminology, the American Sociological Review, and Society for the Study of Social Problems. In addition, she was recently appointed to the Outstanding Scholarship Award Committee of the Crime and Delinquency Division of the Society for the Study of Social Problems.